PRINCIPAL MATTERS
101 Tips for Creating Collaborative Relationships Between After-School Programs and School Leaders

By Paul G. Young

Credits
Editing: Erika Konowalow
Cover and book design: Key Metts

ISBN: 0-917505-23-9
ISBN-13: 978-0-917505-23-2

1. Leadership 2. After-school programs 3. Collaboration 4. Adult learning
5. Building school-community partnerships

Published by School-Age NOTES, P.O. Box 476, New Albany, OH 43054

Table of Contents

Acknowledgments

This book could not have been written without the encouragement, assistance and support of many individuals. Foremost among them are the members of the board of directors and staff members of the West After School Center. Together with the principals, administrators and staff members from the Lancaster City Schools, we strive to attain the highest standards of collaboration and professional performance as described in this book.

My appreciation is extended to those who, for many years, have dedicated their careers to the development and sustainability of outstanding programs for children and youth during out-of-school times. All of us currently working in the field owe them our gratitude and respect.

Principals matter for successfully linking the school day with extended, out-of-school learning opportunities for children. I thank my colleagues across the country who have shared stories and testimonials about how they work effectively with after-school program leaders. I applaud their efforts. They get it!

Every author appreciates an experienced and insightful publisher, editor and designer. When I shared the draft of this book with Tracey Ballas, Erika Konowalow and Kieren Metts at School-Age NOTES, they immediately saw its value for leaders in schools and after-school programs. Because of their professionalism, perseverance and detailed work, the final product is one of shared pride for each of us.

I am honored to have the encouragement and support from the leaders of the National AfterSchool Association and the National Association of Elementary School Principals. Judy Nee and Gail Connelly, and the boards of directors from both national associations, are modeling collaborative practices for their respective memberships. They are visionary thinkers and leaders. They are setting the tone. As a result, a new day for learning will soon become a reality in all our schools.

Last, I am blessed with a wife, two daughters, a son-in-law and a large extended family who understand that learning occurs at all times and in all places. Their unselfish sacrifices have provided me time to reflect, talk, share, write and engage in a variety of professional leadership activities. With their support, and that of my God, all things are possible.

Dedication

This book is dedicated to my wife, Gertrude, my daughter Katie, and my daughter and son-in-law Mary Ellen and Eric Rahn, who continuously inspire, support and encourage learning with everyone they encounter — both in and out of school.

Foreword

"In a new day for learning, there is no final bell."
— *from A New Day for Learning (2007), a report from the Time, Learning, and Afterschool Task Force funded by the C.S. Mott Foundation*

Research shows that effective after-school programming increasingly meets the needs of numerous students and families. Programs that are aligned with the school day provide seamless learning opportunities for children where they can continue to build skills, explore and enrich their learning and develop important mentoring relationships with community volunteers. And best practice shows that continual, effective collaboration between the school principal and the after-school program director is a key ingredient for program success and positive outcomes for children.

We are delighted that Paul Young has expounded upon the after-school program standards of both professional associations and developed this practical, helpful guide for principals and after-school program directors. He knows and understands the challenges in both roles. He has been a leader in both settings. He has served on the board of directors of both associations. His insights and advice will be helpful as principals and after-school program directors work to establish a vision for their programs, ensure quality, advocate and engage stakeholders in the important work of advancing their learning communities. Open it to any page and you will find this book useful. Dr. Young's 101 tips for effective collaboration will guide those who are new to their roles, affirm best practice and provide reflective activities that support professional development.

This book is also timely in that it provides practical, job-embedded guidance for leaders from schools and after-school programs at a time when NAESP and NAA are entering into a deliberate collaborative partnership intended to support the needs of all children in all learning

Principal Matters

communities. Common sense shows that two entities working together can accomplish more than one alone. Two leading national associations, working together to share responsibility for success, will provide greater support and resources for their members — and better outcomes for children.

This book is an example of that spirit of working together and establishing common ground and interests. Read it. Learn from it. Enjoy it. By deliberately collaborating and working together as partners, we can effectively lead the learning day for America's children.

Gail Connelly, Executive Director
National Association of Elementary School Principals

Judy Nee, President/CEO
National AfterSchool Association

Preface

After-school programs are here to stay. Although they may be governed and structured differently, they share a common mission — to provide children with a safe and nurturing environment in which to extend learning past the school day. And a key that makes that environment one in which children and families can achieve numerous benefits is the quality of the collaboration between the principal and the after-school program director.

On face value, that should seem obvious. But the reality is, collaboration is hard work. To reach a high level of effective collaboration requires a vision and an unshakable commitment to a partnership. It requires an understanding of how people inherently process information, learn, communicate, relate, solve problems, contribute to teams, become stressed, maintain health and advance along their path of development. To create a paradigm in which schools and after-school programs are connected to create seamless learning experiences for children requires continuous adult learning and development of collaboration to make it happen.

When I was a teenager, my father used to say to me, "Paul, to get anywhere in life, you have to know where you are going and have a road map that will take you there." He was a master at being able to envision long- and short-term goals and effective strategies that would achieve desired results. He was a farmer and learned what he needed to know and do each day as an apprentice to my grandfather. Practical advice and tricks of the trade of farming had been passed through several generations in our family. My father learned best by watching others and asking numerous "how-do-you-do-that" questions.

Before I became an elementary school principal, I studied theory and practice in rigorous college classes. The credential I earned was recognized by my potential employers as a requirement of a mastery of basic administrative and leadership skills. But once in my first principalship, I faced a steep learning curve. I quickly realized my college classes hadn't prepared me for the unique challenges of a job in the real world. I sought and found support and practical advice from my colleagues, particularly my mentors. I learned how to be a principal by watching others and asking numerous "how-do-you-do-that" questions.

Now, in another exciting phase of my career — leading after-school programs — I find myself facing another steep learning curve and again reaching out and connecting dots with newly identified colleagues for advice, "how-to" practical ideas and support as I clarify a vision, collaborate and lead others in the fulfillment of the mission of the community-based after-school program where I work.

Additionally, because of my experience as a principal and an after-school program director, I am the frequent recipient of "show-me-how" requests for advice about collaboration from those who do what I do every day — lead an after-school program. My peers and I have varied titles, work in diverse settings and come to our jobs from different backgrounds and levels of preparation. But regardless of where we come from or where we work we share common challenges, the most formidable being those of learning how to lead and collaborate with another leader. Having worn both hats, I understand how important it is that principal/program director collaboration take place regularly. I have experienced the power and value of learning and facing challenges as a team. I know that given the right tools, advice and direction, principals and after-school program directors will create remarkable teams capable of creating invaluable learning experiences for children throughout the day.

This book is designed to be a practical handbook for principals and after-school program directors as they work to create those experiences for children. Its contents are conceived to outline important competencies, guide program leaders in a positive direction and map strategies that help them get there. Beyond those key leaders — whose responsibility it is to collaboratively envision and create extended learning opportunities for children — the contents of this book might also provide readers from other diverse backgrounds with special insights into the leadership needs of after-school programs. Together, the contents of this book and ideas from the reader based on interest, experience, involvement and responsibilities for after-school programs will provide vital support for the leaders whose primary charge is to make things happen — after school.

About the Author

Paul Young, Ph.D., a retired elementary school principal, is the executive director of the West After School Center in Lancaster, Ohio. He began his career as a high school band director and then retrained to become a fourth-grade teacher before becoming an elementary principal in 1986.

He served as president of the Ohio Association of Elementary School Administrators (OAESA) in 1997 and was elected to the National Association of Elementary School Principals (NAESP) Board of Directors in 1998 (the only person elected by write-in ballot). He became president-elect in 2001-2002 and served as the national president during the 2002-2003 school year. He retired in December 2004 and since then has served as an advocate for the advancement of equitable and affordable after-school programming for all children. In March 2008, he was selected to become a member of the board of directors of the National AfterSchool Association.

Young completed a bachelor of fine arts degree in music education in 1972 and a master of music degree in trombone performance in 1973, both from Ohio University-Athens. He earned a doctorate in educational administration from OU in 1992. Young has taught undergraduate music classes at Ohio University-Lancaster for more than 25 years and is an advocate for the arts. He is the past president of the Ohio University School of Music Society of Alumni and Friends.

Young is the author of *You Have to Go to School, You're the Principal: 101 Tips to Make it Better for Your Students, Your Staff, and Yourself; Mentoring Principals: Frameworks, Agendas, Tips, and Case Studies for Mentors and Mentees;* and *Promoting Positive Behaviors: An Elementary Principal's Guide to Structuring the Learning Environment.* He also has written numerous articles about music, the arts, after-school programming, student management and the principalship.

Young is married to Gertrude and they have two daughters, Katie and Mary Ellen.

Persuading the Natural Leader

A common assumption from early studies of animal intelligence suggested that sheep, compared with other animals, were slow learners. But on our family farm, my father knew better and helped me understand and appreciate the group flocking and following instincts of sheep as well as their high level of intelligence that researchers are now beginning to affirm.

While serving as a principal, I sometimes felt belittled by others who viewed my strong desire to network with my colleagues coupled with a hesitancy to jump upon the latest fad, trend or educational practice as weak leadership traits. But as with sheep, my colleagues and I learned by observation and acted with discriminate, self-preservation instincts. Now as a trainer, I appreciate others' frustration with the large amount of time it takes for many principals to embrace change.

Yet, what my father taught me while working with our flock of sheep still rings true today. Principals can and will change, perhaps in a painfully slow way, but as a group, they will follow best practice when they clearly see that it is a safe and practical option. To lead our flock of sheep from one field to the next, we often had to steer them around obstacles and through a gate. If we became frustrated, Dad would advise us, "Work with and convince the natural leader to follow you through the gate, and the rest will surely and quickly do the same."

As we work to persuade principals to collaborate with after-school program leaders to extend the learning day for children, the key to success — and the adoption of effective practices by the masses — is to work with and convince natural leaders to go through the gate to a field of better practice. Do that and the others will follow.

Introduction

"There is no greater obligation that we have than to make sure that our kids get a great education before school, during school, and after school."
— *Wisconsin Gov. Jim Doyle*

While I was leading a regional meeting of after-school program directors in my home state of Ohio in the fall of 2007, a young woman who had been newly hired to direct her school-based, middle grades after-school program, and who appeared to be overwhelmed by the information I shared, raised her hand and asked: "Is there any kind of book or guide that you are aware of that outlines everything I am supposed to know and be able to do this year?" Stress was visible in her body language and sounds of frustration audible in the tone of her voice. Immediately, images of books for principals began appearing in my mind, but I was unaware of anything practical for a leader charged with directing an after-school program.

The challenges this young woman faced were numerous. She had been hired to direct the program in late summer after the announcement of the award of a 21st Century Community Learning Center (21stCCLC) grant for the school district. She hadn't been involved in the grant writing process; neither had the school principal. She was creating a program from scratch and staking out turf in a middle school without much support. Everyone around her was preoccupied with other work. The responsibilities of meeting all compliance issues, hiring staff, selecting and recruiting students, and starting and promoting the program were her sole charge. She was re-entering the workforce after being a stay-at-home mom. Her experiences in business and teaching were vastly different than what she was encountering in the after-school field.

It appeared to me that her greatest challenge was developing a collaborative partnership with the principal. She instinctively knew she could learn from me and other practitioners, professionals who faced similar challenges each day. She asked for help so she didn't have to re-create the wheel.

Thus, this book is designed to be a handbook of information and mentoring advice for emerging leaders in after-school education. For those with experience, its contents will affirm best practice. Readers might discover ideas and advice that they shared with me along our mutual professional career paths.

My purpose in writing this book is to share practical advice and professional resources related to collaboration just like what was requested of me during that meeting near the shores of Lake Erie. Its contents are intended to provide insights that can help resolve many of the day-to-day job challenges that principals and after-school program directors face leading after-school programs. The tips are offered to spark reflection, promote professional growth, increase collaboration among leaders and advance the field of after-school education. Readers should easily recognize many common-sense, effective work habits and practices that can be shared, adapted as needed and applied to their work environment. Ultimately, it is hoped that readers will apply what is learned to improve collaboration and create quality learning and social experiences for kids.

As I reviewed professional journals, collected materials from professional associations, surfed online resources, and scanned the inventories of various publishing companies, I began formulating the outline for this book and arranging tips in alignment with the standards books published by the National AfterSchool Association (NAA) and the National Association of Elementary School Principals (NAESP). The 101 tips in this book are not intended to be an exhaustive road map to achievement of those standards but a collection of information and advice that will inspire other ideas, discussion topics, professional sharing and career development.

The standards provide the framework from which key words or phrases are selected to categorize the tips. The book is arranged in ten parts:

Part I —Tips That Help Clarify the Program Vision

Part II — Tips that Enhance Learning

Part III —Tips That Support Principal/Program Director Collaboration

Part IV — Tips That Support Program Organization

Part V — Tips That Assure Quality Program Development

Part VI — Tips That Support Development of Program Infrastructure

Part VII — Tips That Develop Advocacy for After-School Programming

Part VIII — Tips That Support Parent and Community Engagement

Part IX — Tips That Support Personal Care

Part X — Tips That Further Professional Development

One reader might find particular interest in creating the program vision, another in developing the infrastructure. You are encouraged to move throughout the ten parts of the book discovering what most fulfills your adult learning needs. Or, read the book in its entirety then refer back to it often. Regardless, discuss the contents with your collaborative partner, discover better ways of leading change — and share your learning!

In addition to this book, an online component featuring section summaries to be used for self-reflection, charts and sample evaluations can be printed out. These PDFs can be found at www.schoolagenotes.com.

For years, I have stated that nothing effective happens in an elementary or middle level school unless it has the endorsement and support of the principal. It only makes sense that the same applies for the after-school program director. During that time, it is the program director who must lead and set the tone. Working closely together, supporting each other's work, the principal and the after-school program director can connect the learning environment and experiences for children that will help them reach their fullest potential. Their collaborative efforts will fulfill a mission of elevating the educational experience of children to a level higher than they found it.

Paul Young
Lancaster, Ohio
April 2009

Focus on Children

"No significant learning occurs without a significant relationship."
— *Child psychiatrist Dr. James Comer*

Just as principals must make tough decisions during the school day, program directors face them after school. Without fail, situations will develop that pit staff members against parents. Influential community members will question and challenge program policies. Nagging conflicts will persist with adults who choose to challenge the philosophy of after-school programming — and the program director must make decisions that address these and other challenging issues.

Principals and after-school program directors know what it is like when the walls seem to be closing in around them. When the outcomes of the decisions you must make are unclear or the political pressure to appease constituents becomes intense, filter your decision-making processes through what is best for children. Work together. More often that not, the toughest conflicts you will be forced to collaboratively resolve will be the interest-based issues of adults — requests made at the expense of kids. It's easy to succumb to adult peer pressure. But keep your focus on the children's needs.

Your decisions must be based on sound, ethical judgment. When you always weigh the needs of children against the highest ethical standards, your decisions will attain a consistent balance, others will come to view you as a wise and confident leader, you will enjoy peace of mind and know that, in the end, if it's best for children, it's good for your program.

PART I

TIPS THAT HELP CLARIFY THE PROGRAM VISION

The development of an after-school program begins with a dream, a vision of what can be and how future conditions will be better because of the outcomes produced by the program. Sometimes that dream is envisioned by one group and left to be carried out by someone else. Grant writers sketch out promising practices to be implemented by others. Principals may start an initiative only to retire or be transferred. Community-based groups develop partnerships with schools only to find new players in key positions at the beginning of a school year. Visions must be revisited, reshaped, adapted and sometimes changed. Without a clear vision, an after-school program will not prosper, grow or be sustained.

As you begin to develop your collaborative relationship, one of the first items to discuss is the program vision. The principal and the after-school program director must be able to envision the same picture and outcomes. Talk about it. Share it. Help others believe in it. Your vision will guide your work and clarity will produce positive outcomes.

A vision statement describes what your after-school program will ideally look like if it achieves its goals in the coming years. It should resonate with all members of the organization and help them feel proud, excited and part of something much bigger than themselves. A vision should stretch the organization's capabilities and image of itself. It gives shape and direction to the organization's future.

A mission statement is a precise description of what an after-school program (or organization) does. It should describe what the program (or organization) is, why it exists, what it does and define its priorities. Each member of an organization should be able to verbally express it. If an idea surfaces that doesn't align with the mission statement, it shouldn't be considered.

If your personal life mission aligns with that of the organization, you stand a good chance of being happy in your work. If not, you will likely be dissatisfied as the director of any after-school program.

TIP 1

Create a
Powerful Vision

In *The Leadership Challenge,* Kouzes and Posner (1995, p. 95) define *vision* as "an ideal and unique image of the future." To create a vision for an after-school program, the principal and program director must understand the values, beliefs, needs, practices and assumptions of the constituents and key stakeholders that form the school district and the sponsoring organization. If the after-school program is operated by the school district, the vision must be aligned with the vision adopted by the board of education. For nonprofits, the vision is determined by a governing body.

It is the job of the principal and the after-school program director to articulate the vision and help others conceptualize and own it. Both must be passionate about the vision and influence the professional work of subordinates to fulfill expectations and accomplish goals. Without a vision, and leaders who inspire people to share and own it, the after-school program will flounder. Staff members will struggle trying to focus, follow plans and make sense of their work. Parents and students will never achieve buy-in. The program will never achieve greatness.

An organizational or program vision suggests a positive future. To articulate the vision, the program director must:

- build upon experiences and knowledge
- persuade others to imagine and create possibilities and opportunities
- describe the mental picture of a better future that is owned by all stakeholders
- clarify the vision by talking about it in a variety of settings
- analyze and describe the goals, objectives and strategies that must be achieved to realize the vision.

Some after-school program directors assume their positions without extensive experience in leading other people or responsibility for creating a vision for any kind of program. For many, the new leadership position can be their first. If the program vision is already defined, work to refine it and persuade constituents to make it theirs. If a vision statement does not exist, this must be the first item of business. To work without a vision is to simply stab at the dark.

A mission statement describes why your program exists now. A vision statement describes what the program will look like when your work is done. Unless the principal and program director have a clear conceptualization and understanding of both, don't expect results.

TIP 2

Visit
Established Programs

There is no need to re-invent the wheel. Whether you are in the process of envisioning one or already have an established program, a visit to another site will affirm your vision and mission, provide you with new ideas, and establish a collegial network for staff beyond the program leaders. Contact officials in charge of after-school programming in your state department of education or department of human resources for referrals. Talk with other principals and request permission to visit their sites. Connect with presenters at state and national conferences and follow up with visits to their sites. Plan a field trip and invite your key staff to join you on visits to numerous sites. It will be a great investment of time and a positive learning experience for staff members. Ask a lot of questions and observe best practices.

Great ideas are visualized and adapted by sharing with others. Get out and see the great things happening — after school.

TIP 3

Create
Opportunities

"Shoot for the moon. Even if you miss, you'll land among the stars."
— *Anonymous*

There are those in leadership positions who watch things happen, others who make things happen. You want to be associated with the latter.

Athletes know that risks must be taken to gain the advantage against a formidable opponent. Plays must be envisioned and executed that will position the team for a score and a victory. The best coaches skillfully know how to create those opportunities and they've mastered their craft by watching and learning from others. They don't stand by, throw their hands in the air, give up or acknowledge defeat. They make things happen when others show doubt.

To achieve your ideals, the leader's role is to suggest new ideas and create change. Effective leaders influence and persuade others to follow. They encourage people to dream for themselves and to articulate their own mental picture of the vision. But there is risk involved when leaders suggest new ideas or empower people to change behaviors. Leaders acknowledge the risks they must take to effect change and gain a desired advantage. When taking risks, things may not always work smoothly the first time. Strategies are not always foolproof. Concepts are sometimes misunderstood. Mistakes will be made. Reflect, plan and try again. Don't give up. You can't seize opportunities if you do.

Nothing effective happens in an elementary or middle school without the endorsement and involvement of the principal. Likewise, the program director sets the tone for new ideas after school. Effective after-school leaders make things happen.

TIP 4

Clarify
Expectations

It is admirable and desirable to set high expectations. They are interwoven throughout most standards of effective leadership. Expectations describe a standard of conduct or performance. Principals and after-school program leaders are taught that they must set expectations, but despite their efforts to explain them, not everyone gets the message the first time.

As an example, if it is the expectation in your after-school program that students line up quickly, orderly and quietly at the conclusion of a recreational activity, those in supervisory roles must share a common mental image of what that expectation routinely looks like, how it should sound and how long it should take. Where discrepancies occur, the program director must further clarify. Teach the expectation again and again until the desired performance expectations are demonstrated by children and adults.

Set high expectations, talk about them, write them out, post them in visible places, then constantly reflect, reteach and compare the notion of what is expected to the reality of what is happening. In the rush to get things done, don't let expectations get shoved aside.

Because principals and after-school program directors share turf and students in school-based after-school programs, they must spend time clarifying shared expectations that, left undefined, can create conflict and confusion for all constituents. Those discussions should lead to clarity about, at minimum, expectations that address:

- student attire in the after-school program (If hats are outlawed during school, keep them off after school.)
- homework completion
- work habits, motivational and/or rewards systems
- free choice and play time after school
- nutritional content of snacks

- use of equipment
- student and adult conduct
- supervision of students
- parental involvement
- consequences for misconduct

It is unfortunate when students (or adults) are punished for something they failed to understand. Those situations are greatly reduced when the expectations are taught in a variety of ways and repeated numerous times. This is the important work of leaders, and it is a shared collaborative responsibility of the principal and the after-school program director.

TIP 5

Create a Logic Model

A logic model creates a picture of what your after-school program should ultimately look like and should accomplish. Logic models help leaders plan, implement, evaluate and communicate more effectively. Many funders and organizations require logic models. They are graphic representations of a program showing the intended relationships between investments and results.

Elements of an After-School Program Logic Model	
Program goals	What the program is to accomplish
Program elements	Strategies and activities to achieve goals
Program investments	Required time, money, resources and human capital needed to achieve goals
Short-term outcomes	Results to be achieved within months; one year
Long-term outcomes	Results to be achieved after one year; two years, five years; etc
Data sources and evaluation procedures	Types of data used to evaluate program; how and when measurements will be conducted; processes for using data to drive improvement.

Developing a logic model will bring clarity to the vision by providing an outline of the specific strategies necessary to realize it. Logic models help others, especially potential partners, understand the program and its intended expectations and outcomes and how they may fit into the vision and mission.

TIP 6

Develop an
Organizational Chart

Everyone can benefit from a visual understanding of the protocol, hierarchy and chain of command within an organization. An organizational chart shows the structure of an organization and the relationships and relative ranks of its parts and positions/jobs. A sample organizational chart for a school-based after-school program can be represented as such:

A School-Based After-School Program

Board of Education
↓
Superintendent
↓
Principal ←——→ After-School Program Director
↓   ↓
School Staff   After-School Program Staff Members/Volunteers
↓   ↓
Parents   Parents
↓   ↓
Students   Children

A Community-Based After-School Program

Board of Directors
↓
Principal ←——→ After-School Program Director
↓   ↓
School Staff   After-School Program Staff Members/Volunteers
↓   ↓
Parents   Parents
↓   ↓
Students   Children

There are different dynamics in the chain of command between school-owned and school-based programs compared with those operated by community-based organizations that operate in a school. The principal's role has a different set of dynamics when the collaboration involves a partnership with a community-based program off campus from the school. Ownership and responsibility vary in each set-up, and an organizational chart helps all constituents understand the structure. If your after-school program does not have an organization chart, develop one. This model can help you begin.

TIP 7

Know the
Issues, Benefits and Trends

"The structure of the day for American children and youth is more than timeworn. It is obsolete."
— *from A New Day for Learning, 2007, a report from the Time, Learning, and Afterschool Task Force and funded by the C. S. Mott Foundation*

In some communities, a debate still lingers about who should be responsible for the after-school care of our children. Some think it is the responsibility of the parent. Another view is that after-school care is a natural extension of the school's sphere of influence. There are also opinions that it is strictly a domain of a community's social-service agencies. But there is no debate about the necessity of high-quality, before- and after-school care for children.

One of the most serious issues affecting our children is that too many go home alone after school in dangerous neighborhoods to be left alone for too many hours. Add to those unsupervised weekends and summer days and it quickly becomes apparent that out-of-school, at-risk time becomes counterproductive to what occurs during school.

Too much time alone negatively impacts our children's health. Lonely or bored children frequently self-feed and add extra pounds, increasing their risk of being overweight. As increasing numbers of children from poverty are forced to live in urban, volatile neighborhoods, their opportunities for safe, outdoor recreation and exercise are limited. After-school programs provide a haven to help guard against many unstable neighborhood circumstances and distress factors that affect children.

After-school programs help children live healthier, happier lives and the extra time in safe and supervised learning environments complements the important work done in school. Practitioners in the field must advocate for the provision of quality experiences for all children — not just those from families that can afford to pay.

The benefits of quality after-school care are well documented (U.S. Department of Education; U.S. Department of Justice):

- increased learning (reading and math);
- increased rate of quality homework completion;
- improved attendance at school and lower dropout rates;
- less retention, suspension and special-education placement;
- improved behavior and ability to handle conflict;
- decreased likelihood of substance abuse;
- increased opportunities for health and nutrition education;
- increased opportunities for physical fitness activities;
- increased involvement in extracurricular activities;
- increased exposure to career education and adult mentors;
- less time to watch television and self-feed on junk food; and
- more cooperative attitudes, social skills and positive interactions with adults.

Various advocacy groups, such as NAESP and Afterschool Alliance, have estimated the number of children and youth taking care of themselves after school to be nearly 14 million. Even though there has been some support from federal, state and local governments, there continues to be a lack of quality after-school options for many students and their families, especially the working poor or those receiving public assistance. Parent surveys often find that affordable after-school programs are not available, and where they are, options for elementary-aged children far outnumber those for middle-school students and older.

The federal government's 21st CCLC grant programs have provided resources for the development of after-school programs in high-poverty, high-need areas. Not all communities that need grants have received them and sustainability remains a detriment to continuation of services.

Every principal and after-school program director should become familiar with A New Day for Learning (Time, Learning, and Afterschool Task Force, C.S. Mott Foundation, 2007). This report provides an analysis of the changes taking place in our society and how they affect our children. The members of the task force identify how the American public education system is failing to keep up with changes in society and make recommendations for restructuring education for the 21st century.

As our communities become increasingly diverse, technologies change and the amount of information that must be learned further expands. Schools alone can no longer adequately prepare all children for productive citizenship and the skills needed for the workforce. Successful development and preparation of children for the future must be a shared, community responsibility of schools, faith-based organizations, nonprofits, government agencies and private enterprise.

TIP 8

Acknowledge the Value of After-School Programming

It is important that principals acknowledge and articulate to their staffs and stakeholders that after-school programming is more than baby-sitting. Because school-age child-care programs over time have been identified by many names, it is important to clarify for constituents what a contemporary school or community-based after-school program is.

The term *latchkey* has often been used to describe after-school care. It originated as a descriptor for the child who returned from school to an empty home. Community-based after-school programs, where they developed to gather children in safe places, often came to be known as latchkey programs. They often did little more than provide a safe place for children to wait. A coordinated continuation of the school day was not a major focus or goal.

After-school programs are much more. They are a complementary extension of the learning day — before and after school — but not a replication of more school. They are structured so as not to tax the child but rather to motivate, inspire, enrich and support extended learning.

Misconceptions about what after-school programs are, why they exist and why they are needed must be dispelled. Clarifying this new vision and mission of after-school programming need not done at the expense of programs that provide after-school care and youth-development opportunities. Principals and after-school program directors must work together to distinguish the advantages as well as the differences of both. They must advocate for the needs of all children. Creating additional time for children to learn in a structured environment, to close achievement gaps and to explore interests in a different setting than school are needs and opportunities facing every community.

Principal Matters

TIP 9

Envision Effective
Communication Processes

For the after-school program to become tightly connected with and to extend the instructional program of the school day, the principal and after-school program director need to establish a two-way communication system. First, they need to develop a schedule of regular communication between themselves. Second, they need to determine shared processes of providing information to parents, the community and other constituents. Last, they need to remove barriers and encourage teachers and staff members in both programs to communicate and work together to achieve common goals.

The principal must take the lead to assure that communication systems are in place, such as:

- e-mail access and connections between school and after-school staff members;
- Web site links;
- regular shared meetings and professional-development opportunities;
- shared conference time between school and after-school staff members;
- cell phones or walkie-talkies for immediate personal and mutual contact;
- shared lesson plans;
- shared progress reports;
- weekly information shared via staff bulletins and newsletters; and
- access to parent communication and meetings.

In the most optimal situations, after-school staff members' schedules are flexibly arranged so that they are available to observe in teachers' classrooms, review plans and curriculum pacing guides, record special assignments, confer with teachers and prepare extended learning opportunities for specific students.

The principal and the after-school program director must determine processes that address HIPAA (federal privacy regulations) and provide for the sharing of sensitive student data.

The principal can help the after-school program director envision the complexities of school bureaucracies, initiate change and share accomplishments with the broader school community.

Two-way communication works when both parties intentionally share responsibility for success. When one party abdicates their responsibility to communicate, the program is doomed.

Devote adequate time to meet and talk openly with each other every week. The principal and after-school program director can be a powerful team, assets for each other and advocates for children's extended learning opportunities.

TIP 10

Dream **Big**

"The dogmas of the quiet past are inadequate to the stormy present ... As our case is new, so we must think anew, and act anew. We must disenthrall ourselves."
— *Abraham Lincoln*

Dream big. Believe. Commit yourself to what you are doing. Lead. No one else can do it for you.

PART II

TIPS THAT ENHANCE STUDENT LEARNING

Together, principals and after-school program directors can develop learning environments where all students can prosper, especially children from at-risk conditions who need more time, smaller instructional groups or opportunities to explore areas of interest that are not available during school. After-school programs complement the school day; they are not intended to replace the valuable work that goes on during the school day.

As after-school programs grow and evolve to encompass the broad vision of blended learning communities, principals can share many time-honored tips and pieces of advice with after-school program directors and staff that support instruction, learning, development of relationships, common understandings, communication and motivation for all children.

The tips that follow are only a beginning upon which effective leaders can build a large repertoire of strategies and practices that support a high-quality, model after-school program — one of which any community would be proud to call its own.

TIP 11

Don't Create **More School**

> *"Children have more need of models than of critics."*
> — *Carolyn Coats, author*

As after-school programs evolve to support student achievement and increase schools' overall accountability as measured by high-stakes tests required under the No Child Left Behind Act, a natural temptation exists to expand and extend what educators know best — more school. Programs that look like "more school" aren't always purposefully designed that way, but they seem to become such because it is the model that those who work in them know best.

But keep a focus on the needs of every child.

Imagine the young second-grade boy who struggles to learn to read and doesn't grasp the concept of basic math computations. During the typical school day, this child often might be found and observed in classrooms where large peer groups are being asked to complete large amounts of teacher-driven, paper-and-pencil activities. This child is also likely to appear bored, unconfident, fidgety and anxious. Adults identify him as slow. Forced to learn in an environment that is structured in ways that do not accommodate his needs, he shuts down, acts out and becomes disinterested in school. If you ask him, he describes his favorite parts of the school day as physical education, art, music, lunch and recess. He looks forward to the sound of the dismissal bell.

Why place a child in an after-school program that looks like his second-grade classroom? He needs to learn with his hands, work in small groups, experience a positive and encouraging interpersonal relationship with an adult mentor, and select and gain enjoyment from a variety of learning opportunities different from, yet enriching, those experienced in his classroom or home. He needs to develop his strengths, not his weaknesses.

Today, without a doubt, there simply isn't enough time for many kids to learn everything they must know and be able to do in school. The body of knowledge that kids must know increases exponentially, and for those who come to school lagging, it is seemingly impossible to catch up and close their learning gaps in a six- or seven-hour school day. They need more time, but they don't need more of the same. If they get turned off by guided reading groups during school, it's highly unlikely more of the same after school is going to result in significant gains.

Good doctors vary their approach when they realize one treatment doesn't fit all patients. Principals, school teachers, program directors and their staff members must plan and develop different, creative strategies for those learners who "didn't get it" during the day — as well as for those who did.

If an after-school program becomes more school, our efforts, as well intentioned as they may be, will leave thousands of children behind.

TIP 12

Structure Practices for
Supervision and Instruction

When students are given an inch, they'll take a mile. You've probably heard a variation on that idiom before. It's true in the school setting as well as in after-school programs. When children are not adequately supervised they are more likely to engage in undesirable behaviors. Teachers are justified to complain when they see children for whom they have been responsible during the school day running after school without supervision through the building, disregarding rules and school property. This issue, perhaps more than any other, creates stress, headaches and conflict for principals and after-school program directors. If left unaddressed, ineffective supervision issues can create an irreparable rift between the school and after-school program.

It is the responsibility of the after-school program director to set the tone and clarify expectations for the manner in which students are taught and supervised after school. It is particularly important for adherence to the school's rules and procedures to carry over into school-based after-school programs. Inconsistency is confusing to students and parents. Most often, problems develop when the after-school staff members fail to supervise students effectively.

Together, before the after-school program opens, the principal and program director should work with all staff members to assure that common expectations are taught. In particular, training should involve procedures for:

- attendance tracking and expectations for accounting for absences;
- supervising children in restrooms, hallways and eating areas;
- particular challenges of supervision unique to your setting;
- moving children between groups;
- supervising students on field trips;

- supervising students during fitness activities;
- student/parent sign-in and sign-out processes;
- being able to maintain visibility with children at all times;
- teaching positive self-discipline and responsibility;
- administering consequences; and
- developing and reinforcing positive relationships with students.

When structures are in place that address adult expectations for student supervision, and adults are held accountable, most children will respond positively and do what is expected of them. It is good practice to train school and after-school staff members at the same time. Provide frequent updates throughout the year.

The after-school program director must supervise adults and hold them accountable. They are responsible for supervising children. Where there are problems and children's behavior is out of control, the adults likely need better teaching and clarity of expectations.

Preview Concepts;
Build on Strengths

"Failure is delay but not defeat. It is a temporary detour, not a dead-end street."
— *William Arthur Ward, author and teacher*

As so often happens in an elementary-school classroom, some children simply don't relate to or comprehend a particular concept that a teacher is presenting. If a child is experiencing factors that complicate his or her ability to learn, the potential to consistently fall behind, fail and lose interest in school increases. The current emphasis on passing high-stakes tests exasperates many challenged students' desire to succeed and places them at further risk of tuning out to what happens in the classroom and becoming turned off to learning altogether.

But after-school programming can be very beneficial for a child in such a predicament. Once teachers have identified a challenged student, they can encourage and assist with his or her enrollment in the after-school program. They can provide after-school staff members with information about the child's interests and strengths and help provide the child with time to experience success, precious time not always available in classes where brighter students often get things right the first time. Many students come to school with learning experiences that help them grasp new information. Challenged students lack those experiences and an ability to relate. After-school programs provide that extra time.

More important, however, is the necessity that the challenged student be assisted with a difficult concept in an expedient manner. For others, the opportunity to preview concepts, particularly in science and social studies, will enable them to attain a level playing field with their more fortunate peers. The opportunity to preview spelling words a week before they are presented to the class, and to understand the meaning of new vocabulary words and practice using them in sentences can boost the child's confidence in the classroom. Principals have the authority to assure that after-school program staff members gain advance access to what is being taught. After-school program directors have the responsibility to assure that children's needs are met and that they are provided every opportunity to experience success.

Guard against the dangers of the self-fulfilling prophecy. Don't judge or label kids because of what they can't do. Label and evaluate them by what they can do. Encourage their positive capabilities and turn them into strengths. Praise is more motivating and powerful than criticism.

TIP 14

Develop a
Homework
Policy

If there is one expectation or request from teachers and parents, it is that after-school program personnel help students complete their homework. Homework is an important component of many after-school programs, but it should not and cannot become the whole of the system.

Homework policies have been controversial and challenged for decades, by students who refused to do it, from parents who couldn't or wouldn't help with it, and teachers who were frustrated by the concept of homework for a variety of reasons. Moreover, the negative impact that homework incompletion can have upon students' grades is the source of failure and disengagement from learning for far too many children. The expectation that after-school programs will become a place for challenged children to complete all their school assignments is unrealistic and unfair.

Despite the acknowledged problems that homework policies are designed to address, frustration with homework continues to be a common complaint of children and staff members in many after-school programs. Students come to after-school programs with assignments they can't understand and material they can't read. Many fail to understand the connection between homework and what is being taught during school. For too many children and their families, homework is a chore, a time-worn custom and practice with little value or meaning.

Clearly, however, there are some benefits to homework. It helps reinforce what is taught and learned in school and is a sound practice for developing skills. Monitoring homework is an effective practice that helps parents become engaged in their children's learning and a way to monitor their progress. Homework reinforces the concepts of self-discipline, organization, responsibility, work and independence.

Principals must take the lead in developing a homework policy for their school. They must:

- develop policies based on research and effective practice;
- work with teachers to clarify what homework should be, establish reasonable time expectations for its completion, and monitor the practice and effectiveness of policies; and
- work with the after-school program director to develop mutual expectations that are sound, realistic and conform to best practice for after-school programming.

Together, principals, teachers, after-school program directors and their staff members must convey those expectations to parents when children are enrolled in the after-school program. It is imperative that professionals work together to teach children and parents the value and meaning of homework and assure them that it is an effective learning practice.

Homework has always been a source of frustration and conflict that sours relationships between the school, the after-school program and the community. When principals and after-school program directors address this issue, it is imperative that they work as a team, understanding the vision and purpose of assignments outside of school and support the value of homework requirements as a way to help children learn and achieve.

Use
Volunteers (Mentors)

Volunteers can provide immeasurable support in an after-school program. The benefits range from simply providing an extra set of hands for completing predetermined tasks to mentoring students and spreading public relations about the program throughout the community. Because of the numerous and varied interpersonal networks that each individual possesses, the return on investment of time to train and work with volunteers can reap huge benefits in resources, community partnerships, advocates and one-on-one support for students.

Effective volunteer programs are guided by policies and procedures that protect the interests of the volunteers, paid staff members and the after-school program. Volunteer programs work best where there is evidence of good planning, coordination and supervision. Before you start a volunteer program, visit a site where volunteers are used. Ask questions. Observe volunteers at work and discuss the needs, processes and challenges of volunteer program implementation with the coordinator.

Effective volunteer programs have an assigned staff member designated as the frontline contact. That individual is responsible for (or delegating):

- recruiting activities;
- answering questions and providing answers for prospective volunteers;
- screening, interviewing, handling applications and assessing strengths and interests;
- checking references;
- providing orientation, tour of facility and explanation of confidentiality issues;

- completing background checks and other requirements along with registration materials;
- scheduling;
- preparing and clarifying assignments;
- training;
- matching students with adults;
- supervising volunteers; and
- recognizing and celebrating volunteer contributions.

Volunteers can be found everywhere. Recruit them from high schools, colleges, businesses, civic and community service groups, government agencies, faith-based organizations, senior citizen centers, assisted-living facilities, nursing homes and parent and family sources. Your list of potential sources for volunteers can go on and on. Regardless if your program is located in a rural, suburban or urban area, you can recruit volunteers if you plan effectively, advertise and make it an ongoing effort. The mission of after-school programming is an easy sell. Just make sure that volunteers are welcomed and shown respect. Assure volunteers that their time is valuable and appreciated. Be sensitive to their needs and tolerant of their inexperience. Teach them. Always plan and prepare meaningful work. Provide warm fuzzies. Help volunteers recognize and celebrate progress, especially those who work as mentors with children.

As individuals from the baby-boomer generation reach their retirement, a vast pool of volunteers should "come of age" in your community. Welcome them to your volunteer program and reap the benefits of their experience and skills.

For more information on developing and managing a volunteer program, review the resources available from the Free Management Library at: http://www.managementhelp.org/staffing/outsrcng/volnteer/volnteer.htm

TIP 16

Sing, Sing, Sing

College-bound seniors with school music experience scored 57 points higher on the verbal portion of their SATs and 41 points higher in math (98 points combined) than those without arts instruction.
Profiles of SAT and Achievement Test Takers, The College Board, 2001

If we have a headache, we think nothing of seeking relief by taking an aspirin. People commonly search out all sorts of quick fixes and medications for a variety of their ailments and health benefits, practices supported by medical research as well as common folk cures.

Research on music and its impact on the developing brain, popularized in our culture as the "Mozart Effect," has created interest in classical music education in the past decade. If we could find a safe, quick fix that increased intelligence, wouldn't everyone want it? Music can be that fix. Even though there are challenges to the research findings that show positive correlations between music exposure and brain development, the fact remains that music is good for kids and should be an integral component of after-school programming. As school leaders reduce students' opportunities to study music, art, drama and other "extras" in an effort to create more time for reading and math instruction, the need for music in after-school programs has never been higher.

Principals and teachers who influence decisions that limit kids' musical studies fail to understand or acknowledge the spatial learning that children experience when they sing. The act of group singing engages children in the environment around them. Singing supports language development. It exercises the lungs and facial muscles and supports one's ability to listen, articulate and engage in conversation. It benefits self esteem, confidence, concentration and emotions. It enhances mood and reduces stress. Singing promotes socialization, creativity, understanding of cultures and healing.

Don't we want all children to acquire these human skills just as much, or more, than reading and math skills? What you will find is that where students are engaged in the arts and stick with it, their attention span, self-control and social behavior increase and they enjoy learning and being in school. Kids with those skills will be happy — making all of our programs succeed. Success after school may be no more elusive than creating more time to sing.

Learn more about the Music Makes You Smarter research at the American Music Conference Web site: www.amc-music.org.

TIP 17

Teach **Languages**

Learning to read is an overarching goal for students in after-school programs. To read, students need to learn to speak the language and also understand the visual representation of letters, words and sentences. If the child comes from a home where English is spoken, they've likely been learning and preparing for school by hearing and reading English since they were infants. But for the increasing number of children in after-school programs who hear other languages in their homes, having nurturing adults to help them learn English during and after school is invaluable to their future success in this country.

Principals and after-school program directors should incorporate the study of languages other than English in their programs. Most young children can learn a second language easily and they also benefit from the study of other cultures, traditions and geography. The emphasis in schools to raise test scores has driven much of the time for the study of extras out of the curricula. Thus, after-school programs are a logical place for students to learn second languages. After-school programs exist to complement and extend children's learning opportunities.

Invite volunteers to teach groups of children a second language and to share information about the other cultures. Develop weekly or monthly themes and encourage everyone in the center to learn a new language — even adults. Wonderful partnerships will develop that will support your mission. Children will experience a learning opportunity they might not receive elsewhere. They will learn to understand other people and understand their world from an enlightened perspective.

Teaching languages does not require a significant amount of time each day. However, students should have consistent exposure to the language, hear tape recordings of the language being spoken and continue to learn over an extended period of time. Bilingual children will enjoy benefits not available to English-only speakers.

Part II: Tips That Enhance Student Learning　　　　　　　　**47**

Teach
Typing

Typing skills are important for children who will work with keyboards and computers in their educational and work experiences. But because of the time required to prepare students for high-stakes tests, the development of typing skills is left for many children to learn on their own.

Decades ago, typing was taught in most high schools. Many vocational courses of study required typing skills. Children today can't afford to wait until high school. They are introduced to computers in preschool, and without proper training and adequate time to practice and develop their skills, they likely will develop bad habits that can inhibit their productivity at the keyboard.

Learning to type is not just about developing mechanical skills. By teaching typing, after-school staff members can reinforce school learning objectives and extend the learning day. It won't appear to children to be a repeat of more of the same lessons they had at school. Typing is an excellent way to reinforce:

- reading, spelling and punctuation skills;
- concentration and self-discipline;
- development of speed when reading and writing;
- use of technologies;
- presentation of work at higher standards; and
- independence and preparation for the workforce.

Principals and after-school program directors should ensure that access to computers and computer labs is made available for children and staff members in the after-school program. Along with developing conversational second language skills, learning to type should be another learning experience that all children can enjoy — and use as an adult.

TIP 19

Promote Good
Nutrition and Fitness

The increasing incidence of childhood obesity has placed the issue among the most serious medical concerns facing children. Childhood obesity is troubling because extra pounds place children at higher risk of diabetes, high blood pressure and high cholesterol. Extra pounds gained before the teen years are difficult to take off — if they ever are. Simply put, most of our children eat too much and don't get enough exercise. On the other side of the problem are those children who don't have enough to eat. Principals and after-school program directors must address the needs of all children. And for hungry kids, much of their daily intake of food is provided at school and after school.

The typical school lunch has become a scapegoat as the source of children's consumption of fatty, starchy junk foods. But that is unjustified. Principals and after-school program directors must challenge and correct that perception with facts. School lunches and snacks served in public schools and licensed programs must meet stringent guidelines established by the U.S. Department of Agriculture. Daily menus must contain prescribed numbers of servings from the basic food groups and may not exceed established portion sizes for children. If children eat no more than what is served during the school breakfast, lunch and after-school snack and supper programs, assuming they do not have a hormonal or medical condition, it is highly unlikely they would gain excessive weight. In fact, with exercise, they would most likely maintain normal body weight.

Success in any weight management program is determined by one's ability to make good choices. Education is the key. Principals and after-school program directors must assure that their curricula contains nutrition education. They should engage children in cooking activities, teach an understanding of food labels and dietary needs and help them learn to make good choices. Moderation is the key to making good choices over time.

There are many benefits to be gained from walking. It's an inexpensive exercise and can help children:

- gain more energy;
- develop toned muscles that contain less body fat;
- reduce stress;
- sleep better;
- develop healthier bones and joints; and
- reduce their risk for heart disease, diabetes, colon cancer, stroke, high blood pressure and osteoporosis (Arizona Board of Regents, 2005).

Most likely, you are already well versed about the dangers of increasing childhood obesity and the benefits of exercise. However, you might not have had a discussion or reached mutual agreement about how the issues should be addressed after school. Perhaps you have yet to experience a challenge from parents who do not want their children involved in walking programs or others who choose to send sugary drinks and fattening treats to the after-school program. Conflict quickly develops and mixed messages are sent to parents when procedures and expectations are different between what happens during and after school. Without wellness and food-service policies that extend to the after-school program, it is hard to provide clear direction and stand firm as a team when challenged.

Make sure issues about health and nutrition are addressed in your parent handbook. Use the information contained within this tip when speaking to parents and other constituents.

TIP 20

Develop a Program
for Summer
Learning

Teachers commonly complain that many students lose academic progress during the summer. It requires weeks to regain proficiency of skills and habits that become dormant over a two- or three-month period. Some students never close the gaps. Summer learning programs provided by after-school staff members can provide the continuous learning experiences and link between spring and autumn classes that students and parents desire.

A good summer program includes:

- nutritious lunches and snacks;
- outdoor fitness activities, especially swimming;
- variety of arts classes and extended experiences within the community;
- field trips to museums, libraries and places of historical interest;
- opportunities to explore areas of the curriculum not available in the school year;
- remedial activities in reading and math and/or enrichment;
- technology education;
- guest speakers; and
- opportunities for play and social development.

Learning never stops. Kids need opportunities to continue their learning in a safe and structured environment. This is the time during which many students can close their achievement gaps. Work to ensure that your after-school program continues during the summer months.

TIP 21

Teach
Perseverance

"The difference between perseverance and obstinacy is that one often comes from a strong will, and the other from a strong won't."
— Henry Ward Beecher

What is perseverance? It is commitment, hard work, patience, endurance. It is being able to bear difficulties calmly and without complaint. Kids with perseverance skills are willing to try and try again. Children who understand what perseverance means and have role models who display those skills can gain an advantage over their peers who give up quickly. Perseverance skills can become an asset as children become young adults and enter the workforce.

Children's efforts can be reinforced with a variety of statements when facing challenges:

- Always finish what you start.
- When something doesn't work right, try again and again.
- Don't give up on difficult jobs or situations.
- Work a little harder or a few minutes longer on a task that you do not like.
- When something starts to bother you, wait as long as you can before you express frustration.
- Don't lose your temper when something upsets you.
- Focus on issues, not personalities, when you lose your patience and try to understand it (and don't "lose it").

Principals and after-school program directors will find that children who are supported and encouraged to develop perseverance skills will do better in the classroom. All kids need instruction in this life skill, but like many other intangible parts of the curricula, it often takes a back seat to teaching and practicing reading and math. After school is an appropriate place, a nurturing place and a safe place for children to learn academic and social skills that will equip them for success in life.

And of course, principals and after-school program directors must possess highly developed perseverance skills to succeed in their jobs. Don't miss the opportunities to sit with children and explain your stories of perseverance. Your example could become the motivation needed for a young child to change behavior.

TIP 22

Teach **Manners**

"Before we can conquer the world we must be able to conquer ourselves."
— *Alexander the Great*

Just like perseverance, children gain an advantage when they grow up learning how to display good manners, demonstrate common acts of courtesy and observe basic rules of etiquette. Employers may be able to teach or remediate reading and math skills, but they likely won't tolerate workers who disregard or disrespect others in the workforce. In the short term, teachers also are more inclined to build positive relationships with children who display manners. Teaching manners to students in after-school programs, and getting observable results, can go a long way in developing positive school-home-community-after school relationships.

After-school program staff members should be observed actively engaging children in lessons that help them display:
- pleasant and respectful greetings (smile and make eye contact; learn to give and receive a proper handshake);
- use of words such as *please* and *thank you*;
- common etiquette (hold the door for others; don't interrupt; show respect for elders; say *yes* instead of *yeah*, *may I* instead of *can I*, never use *ain't*);
- understanding of how to share, take turns and listen;
- good table manners;
- proper ways to give and receive compliments;
- proper ways to give and receive criticism;
- respectful relationships with adults;
- respectful relationships with other children;
- respect for different cultures;
- respect for individuals with disabilities;
- respect for property; and
- good sportsmanship.

TIP 23

Ensure
Safety

Standards for high-quality after-school or school-age child-care programs state that the assurance of student safety should be a prime concern. And effective principals and after-school program directors strive to achieve safety every day, for the children and the adults under their watch.

Safety plans also encompass security measures. Obviously, quality programs must meet compliance regulations to assure that physical hazards have been removed from the program environment. They must also focus on the nonphysical dangers that are always changing and being perpetrated by human beings of all ages. Supervision practices and expectations must be taught, continually observed, reinforced and evaluated.

A quality safety and security plan should be designed to fit the specific needs, setting and environment of each after-school program. The plan should be reviewed by community authorities, written, posted, distributed, practiced and continually reviewed for effectiveness.

The plan should include:

- student-supervision strategies and expectations;
- procedures for taking attendance and notifying parents of absences;
- procedures and expectations for maintaining security of windows and outside doors;
- strategies for preventing access to the school or center of all unauthorized people;
- emergency contact numbers for community safety forces;
- emergency contact information (for students and adults);
- emergency evacuation plans and identification of alternative relocation sites;
- location of medical first-aid kits and procedures to address children's medical needs;
- inspection procedures and maintenance of outside play areas;

- inspection procedures and maintenance of indoor program areas;
- routine cleaning practices and procedures and assurance of healthful preparation of foods; and
- hand-washing procedures and expectations.

These items are by no means comprehensive. Add or subtract to meet the needs of your unique program. For programs that are housed in school buildings, align your standards and safety and security plans with those that the principal enforces during the school day — assuming they meet licensing and grant regulatory standards. Don't assume they do, and if you are not in agreement, schedule time to address the issue with the principal. Safety and security are issues that may pose different requirements between school and after-school personnel — even if it is the same location.

Safety and security are daily responsibilities for program administrators. Students cannot learn if they are afraid or there is threat to their welfare. Be observant and vigilant in your efforts to prevent potential harm.

PART III

TIPS THAT SUPPORT PRINCIPAL/ PROGRAM DIRECTOR COLLABORATION

Principals and after-school program directors know that connecting what children learn during school and after school adds valuable learning time, boosts achievement and develops happier, healthier learners. But when a principal's plate is already full and more is always being placed on it, the thought of extending the workday to include an after-school program can appear to be an overwhelming task, adding more stress instead of reducing it. If it appears that the after-school program director lacks important skills and competencies, busy principals might view after-school program development to be more trouble than it's worth. But working alone can be much more taxing than working with a partner, even one who might need to be trained.

There are several key individuals who contribute to a principal's success on the job: an understanding and supportive spouse and family; an efficient and faithful administrative assistant; and a capable, reliable and trustworthy assistant principal. However, when those individuals lack key supportive skills and abilities, they quickly become liabilities for the principal rather than assets.

In smaller schools, assistant principals are uncommon. Principals who lack assistance often complain about stress, excessive workloads and long hours. But when an after-school program is structured in ways that genuinely support the school, the extra set of hands are personified by the after-school program director.

Don't misunderstand. Assistant principals and after-school program directors fulfill very different roles. But, from the overworked principal's perspective, in a school unlikely ever to afford an assistant principal, the after-school program director can provide assistance in many valuable ways by sharing responsibility for:

- data collection, management and analysis;
- student management and social development;
- parent engagement;
- technology support;
- public relations; and
- conflict management.

Why? How? Effective after-school program directors deal with the above items and more, and they deal with them in many of the same ways that principals do because they work with many of the same students and adults. It is only logical that work should be shared that leads to the mutually desirable outcomes — happier, healthier students and families who are excited about learning and their involvement in school.

Just like with principals, after-school program directors need to be surrounded by an encouraging family and stellar employees and most important, a capable, reliable and trustworthy principal with whom to work. A respectful relationship between principals and after-school program directors can be very powerful and motivate others to work together to share responsibility for success. But placing two individuals together and expecting them to plan, share information, solve problems, support each other and get along is much easier said than done. It requires an intentional effort from both, an understanding of collaboration and a willingness to accept advice and be open to change.

The contents of this section are intended to help principals and after-school program directors define their roles, understand each others' jobs, and learn to work together as a team.

TIP 24

Define **Collaboration**

The development of effective after-school programming requires that principals and after-school program directors work closely together. But before they begin working together in a collaborative partnership, they must study, define and understand what it means to collaborate.

Collaboration is broadly defined as a structured act or process where two or more people work together toward a common goal. That goal is typically an intellectual endeavor and creative in nature. The word collaboration is used interchangeably with teamwork, cooperation, partnership and joint venture. Collaboration does not mean that one individual, using positional power, influence or authority, dominates the other. Instead, collaboration works when participants realize each can't succeed without the other. A collaborative relationship is characterized by trust, collective power and authority, shared information, teamwork and an ability to resolve conflicts. At its best, adult collaboration is a satisfying and rewarding experience for all participants — and produces positive experiences for children.

As a partnership between a principal and after-school program director develops, it will go through several typical stages of development as described in the literature of organizational change. They are commonly known as the:

- forming period — where the participants get to know each other and agree on purpose;
- storming period — where positions, roles, norms and strategies are defined;
- norming period — where the work gets done; and
- performing period — where assessment, evaluation and reflection take place.

The attitudes and activities of the principal can have a dramatic impact on the success of any collaboration. A supportive principal typically allows leadership and responsibility to be shared and makes collaboration a priority. The principal who is not supportive tends to be passive and uninvolved and exhibit behaviors that can undermine the collaboration. Collaboration requires effort from two or more participants. After-school program directors must fulfill their commitments to the process as well.

The rubric in Figure 24a (available at www.schoolagenotes.com) is designed as a self-assessment progress guide outlining key collaborative activities for individuals engaged in after-school program implementation.

Self-assessment scores are prone to be lowest or most inaccurate as collaborators go through the storming stage. During that stage, when controversies and significant disagreements arise, individuals often want to see things as being better than they really are. Later, during the norming stage, work gets done and collaborators more honestly reflect on their contribution to mutual projects.

Successful collaboration requires a strong commitment to face-to-face professional learning. Anything less is contrived and doomed to disintegrate in conflict.

An Example of Collaboration That Works

Stephanie, principal of Main Street Elementary School, could be described as a visionary leader. When approached by Philip, the CEO of a nonprofit community organization, she saw the opportunities that collaboration would provide and played an active role in writing the 21st Century Community Learning Center Grant for the school-based program that Philip's organization was eventually awarded to operate.

To ensure that the program was implemented effectively, Stephanie worked closely with Philip to recruit and hire a competent site director. She invited Philip and the after-school program site director to staff meetings, encouraged her interested staff members to apply for instructional positions in the after-school program and established guidelines and memorandums of understanding that addressed curricula, program structure, turf, and student selection and management.

Most of all, Stephanie continually viewed the after-school program as an extension of the school and included Philip as the school's closest partner. She became a cheerleader and community advocate for increased after-school opportunities.

To ensure that their collaborative partnership worked effectively and could be sustained over time, Stephanie and Philip agreed to meet weekly to plan, address issues, review data and clarify the vision and expectations.

TIP 25

Create and Use a
Job Description

Unfortunately, there are after-school program directors who work without an officially written description of the responsibilities or requirements of their job. If you are one of those individuals, use the model in Figure 25a (available at www.schoolagenotes.com). Where job descriptions do exist, sometimes they are very generic and have been modified from other administrative or supervisory positions in the school district.

After-school program director positions are different types of administrative positions and must be well defined. A job description is an important collaborative agreement that lists and guides expectations. Don't work without one.

Develop a
Memorandum of Understanding

Memorandums of understanding (MoU) describe agreements between parties. They may or may not be binding legal documents, but just like contracts, they are professionally prepared statements of intent and expectation. It is particularly important for community-based organizations that sponsor school-based after-school programs to have written agreements that clearly outline service deliverables, mutual responsibilities and the use of space, equipment, curriculum materials and other resources.

Memorandums of understanding are effective documents that can be used when planning and developing community partnerships. Better than a gentleman's agreement, a well conceived and well-written document will help diffuse misunderstandings and provide written clarity for assumptions and expectations.

If your school and after-school program do not share a memorandum of understanding, the model in Figure 26a (available at www.schoolagenotes.com) might be helpful in developing one to fit your unique situation and needs.

Meet Regularly and
Use the NAESP Planning Tools

It is important that the principal and the after-school program director meet often to reflect and talk about the program vision and also to
outline responsibilities that support the program infrastructure. In *Leading After-School Learning Communities* (2006), the National Association
of Elementary School Principals (NAESP) has provided principals and
after-school program directors with a valuable set of planning tools to
help do just that. The tools help leaders reflect on practices and decisions
that impact:

- common expectations;
- lines of authority;
- access and distribution of resources;
- budget development and monitoring processes;
- program management and procedures for reviewing concerns;
- accessibility and visibility of leaders;
- sharing of information;
- communication techniques;
- development of a positive culture; and
- goals and outcomes.

Don't reinvent the wheel. Get copies of *Leading After-School Learning
Communities* from NAESP and use the planning tools to guide the reflective meeting agendas that leaders should mutually develop at least once
a month.

TIP 28

Don't Let
Collaboration Be Derailed

In *Dealing with Difficult People* (2006), authors Dr. Rick Brinkman and Dr. Rick Kirschner describe the ten most unwanted behaviors that are exhibited by difficult people as:

- the tank — pushy, ruthless, loud and forceful;
- the sniper — attacks with sabotage, gossip and putdowns;
- the grenade — explodes in tantrums;
- the know-it-all — will talk for hours and won't listen to ideas he thinks are inferior;
- the think-they-know-it-all — will purposely mislead if others are unaware of information;
- the yes person — quick to agree, slow to deliver; will over-promise to please;
- the maybe person — procrastinates until it is too late;
- the do-nothing person — provides no feedback;
- the no person — drives others to despair; always sees a dark lining; negative, unrealistic; and
- the whiner — everything is wrong, drags others down with the weight of generalizations.

Principals and after-school program directors will encounter people who exhibit these behaviors. The tank, the sniper and the know-it-all are overly controlling. The whiner, the no person and the nothing person are pessimistic and perfectionist. It is challenging to seek approval from the passive nothing person, the wishy-washy yes person and the indecisive maybe person. Most people want to be heard and appreciated, and when they feel they are being ignored, they ratchet up difficult behaviors to gain attention.

Everyone reacts differently to people exhibiting difficult behaviors.

Leaders need to be trained to identify the behaviors so that effective responses can be used in particular situations. Everyone can be difficult at times — even principals and after-school program directors. Don't allow difficult behaviors to derail your collaboration efforts. Talk about the difficult behaviors you observe between yourselves and others. Focus on issues. Work to bring out the best in people and each other.

An Example of Collaboration That Does Not Work

Anita had worked in a neighboring school district as a Title I supervisor before moving to High Point City Schools to become the director of Federal Programs with added responsibility for after-school programs. At High Point, she had worked three years with principals and community partners to develop flourishing after-school programs in six of the districts' elementary and middle schools.

Before becoming superintendent of High Point City Schools, Harold had been the high school principal in the same district where Anita had worked. She had been at High Point only two years when Harold suddenly became her boss.

Harold had no experience with after-school programming and little background with elementary curriculum. Anita worked to keep him informed and aware of the positive results of the after-school programs, but he showed only courtesy acknowledgement.

In February, Anita was informed that her after-school programs were operating at a $20,000 deficit and that two community partners had approached board members complaining that their invoices were not being promptly paid. In typical tank behavior, Harold became upset and accused Anita of negligent performance and shared his dissatisfaction with this situation with the board.

But Anita knew she'd done what she was supposed to do and had the self-confidence to uncover the facts. In their former district, she knew it was Harold who had been slow to process invoices and paperwork, and it didn't require much investigation to discover that his ineffective attention to detail authorizing transfers of funds had caused the cash-flow problems for which he now blamed Anita.

Anita assessed the situation of having Harold as her boss. She figured her options were to quit, fight back or find a way to work with and around Harold without causing additional issues that could affect the after-school programs or her job security.

Anita chose to attend every board of education meeting. She never challenged Harold in public, but she also never allowed inaccurate information about her programs to be shared with the board. With her presence near the front row, Harold knew he could never get away with bullying or use her as a scapegoat for his oversights.

Anita never enjoyed a close, professional, collaborative working relationship during Harold's two years as superintendent. She also never again allowed her after-school programs to be compromised.

Her tenacity enabled children and families to prosper and grow.

TIP 29

Present a
Unified Front

Tip 28 describes the importance of understanding and identifying the types of difficult behaviors that leaders encounter when working with people. Moreover, leaders need to be sensitive to how their own difficult behaviors may impact the way others react to them and how their time and effort dealing with difficult behaviors can consume energies better spent on program development.

Just as children may try to get what they want by playing mom against dad, difficult parents and others who feel their interests have been compromised will attempt to play the principal and the after-school program director against each other. When this happens, and both leaders allow their relationship to become compromised, time must be devoted to solving the problem and repairing the relationship. Challenges to the program, to one's authority or one's decisions are best discussed behind closed doors.

Strong relationships are powerful, respectful and motivating. When either partner allows a person exhibiting difficult behaviors to discredit the other, the person with the difficult behavior will maximize that crack in the relationship for their own benefits and interests.

Sometimes, difficult behaviors are personified by other staff members. Teachers and teacher unions can put tremendous pressure on principals to get what they want, sometimes at the expense of what is best for children. When a contractual grievance develops that places the school at odds with the after-school program, the pressure on the principal to affect change can become relentless. At that crucial time, a do-nothing principal creates stress and, in the worst cases, irreparable harm to the relationship.

Throughout history, the phrase "united we stand, divided we fall" has been used in songs and mottos to describe loyalty. Be a reliable partner and be steadfast in your team act. Without a unified front, forces will "divide and conquer" your collaborative partnership.

Make Your Partner
Look Good

Be positive. Principals and after-school program directors must not talk badly about each other. When stressors complicate your collaborative efforts, avoid the temptation to vent with a teacher or staff member. What you say will only be passed along and twisted way beyond its meaning by the time it is inevitably heard by the source of your frustration. Be intentional about saying things to each other that you feel compelled to say to others. Showing a public display of professional respect and privately discussing differences supports a collaborative partnership. It is the ethical way to act. If you can't say something nice, it is better to say nothing at all.

The politics in a school district can be very complex. Decisions are often made at upper levels of the administration that can be difficult to understand at the school level. Principals report to superintendents and the school board and must deal with affairs within their school as a middle manager. Sometimes they do not have the power to influence decisions in ways that are understood by those they work with. For after-school program directors to criticize and speak badly about those difficult decisions serves no purpose other than to seed the "grapevine" with negativity.

Focus on issues rather than personalities. Work to remain loyal to each other and demonstrate courtesy and professional respect. Complaining and talking badly about others accomplishes nothing.

Acknowledge the
Partnership

Principals sometimes forget to acknowledge the contributions of the after-school program when listing community partnerships with their school. In situations where the after-school program is sponsored by a community organization, this oversight can be devastating, embarrassing and hard to correct. Even when the program is owned and sponsored by a school, principals must make it a practice to acknowledge the benefits and contributions of their after-school program and its staff members.

Tell personal stories of how the program affects your students, their families, your work and that of teachers. But be genuine. People can see through a façade.

Principals also appreciate and respond positively to warm fuzzies. After-school program directors should never miss an opportunity to acknowledge the shared vision and support they receive from an effective principal.

Be a
Team Player

"Management must speak with one voice. When it doesn't, management itself becomes a peripheral opponent to the team's mission."
— *Pat Riley*

Team-building develops more easily when principals and after-school program directors work together on tasks of mutual importance. Common work settings and challenges allow leaders to share their collective technical knowledge and skills, solve problems, complete projects and develop programs. While working together and supporting each other, leaders committed to a team effort often develop and articulate guidelines that lead to increased productivity and cooperation.

Effective partnerships between principals and after-school program directors possess common characteristics. They are:

- contributions from each leader;
- a high level of interdependence between each leader;
- an awareness that each leader can influence the team agenda;
- good people skills and a commitment to a team approach;
- a relaxed climate for communication;
- development of mutual trust;
- willingness to share risks;
- clarity about goals and targeted outcomes;
- clearly defined roles and responsibilities;
- an ability to examine errors without personal attacks; and
- a capacity to create ideas.

Teams are a common concept with most people. Most of us can identify teams that do not work well together. But developing a strong team is not something that each of us readily knows how to do. It takes a willing commitment, an attitude of give and take and a realization that two heads are better than one. Until each participant is capable of accepting the other as an equal partner, a team concept will remain an elusive idea.

What Would You Do If This Happened to You?

Mary Beth was hired to direct an elementary-school-based after-school program. The veteran principal of the school, Angela, was a moderate supporter of after-school programs. The program had been expanded because of grant funds obtained for the program by a federal grants administrator in the district. Greater expansion resulted in more classrooms being used in the program.

By mid-January, Mary Beth began picking up on numerous side comments from teachers about how they thought the after-school program was nothing more than free baby-sitting. Disturbed, Mary Beth met with Angela and proposed several ideas to address the perception that teachers had of the program. Her brainstormed ideas included:

- a presentation at a staff meeting to clarify expectations;
- an open invitation for Angela to observe the work being done after school;
- a survey of teachers to obtain feedback on their perceptions of the program;
- a private conversation with the teachers who were making negative comments;
- reports to teachers demonstrating students' improved work as a result of their after-school program participation;
- mobilization of parents to speak with teachers about their satisfaction with the after-school program;
- monitoring of shared turf to eliminate any issues teachers might have about sharing space and resources;
- weekly collaborative planning meetings with Angela to discuss and address this issue and any others; and
- recruitment of school staff members to work in the after-school program.

What additional ideas would you present if this happened to you? How do you think some of Mary Beth's ideas might be improved? What ideas might you not suggest and why? What might be done to make Angela an avid rather than moderate supporter of after-school programs?

Encourage

Involvement of School Staff Members

Principals know that one of their most important tasks is that of hiring good teachers. Hire the best and the rest is easy. The same rings true for after-school program directors.

Many issues related to linking after-school and school programs are minimized when school teachers are employed to work in the after-school program. These individuals know the children, their parents and the curriculum and possess a repertoire of special instructional strategies that help children learn. Encourage their participation in a variety of ways as their time allows. Other teachers are less likely to complain about an after-school program using their turf when they see their colleagues actively involved.

Many people prefer to work a typical seven- or eight-hour workday — but not all. Others elect to work extended periods of time. Consider what they have to offer the program. But be wise. Good people do good work and create good programs. Hire the best for the after-school program.

TIP 34

Be **Visible**

Principals send a strong message about the value of their after-school programs when they drop by frequently. During frequent walk-throughs they can monitor program progress, encourage students, staff members and volunteers and establish a spirit of goodwill. Principals also gain insights into the special needs of challenged learners and their families. They also acquire a unique view of their school, from the outside in, by listening to what volunteers share about their experiences and perspectives working with children after school.

Likewise, it is important for after-school program directors to be visible at the school. Teachers and classified staff members need to become familiar with the after-school program leader, to develop working relationships on their turf and to hear about the program goals and outcomes from the person in charge. Get out and about. Reach out to people. Help them understand the valuable contribution that the after-school program makes for their school. Many issues can be resolved before they become problems simply by being visible, listening and showing people that you care.

TIP 35

Be Inclusive of
Thinking and Needs

Principals need to copy their after-school program directors with important communications and information. They should request the program director's attendance at staff meetings and parent conferences and encourage participation in important decision-making processes. Before developing schedules and finalizing decisions, the principal should contemplate how the outcomes might impact the after-school program, its needs, the learning opportunities for children and the work conditions of the staff. Likewise, after-school program directors should not plan or make decisions that might impact the school without first discussing matters with the principal.

Neglect or insensitivity to this issue will negatively impact collaborative efforts. To be inclusive requires a deliberate mindset — from both individuals. Set a positive example for all who work with you.

TIP 36

Respect the **Property of Others**

When principals are bombarded each morning with complaints from staff members such as "The kids in the after-school program got into my desk" or "The trash cans were not dumped again" or "Someone forgot to shut a window in Room 4," it doesn't take long to ask "Is it worth all the hassle to have the after-school program in the school?"

After-school program directors and principals must teach students and staff members to respect school property and that of individuals. Don't borrow items unless permission has been granted. If something breaks, tell someone about it and be prepared to take responsibility for fixing it.

Teach children what items they may use after school, where they may use them and how. Clean up afterward. Put things back where you found them. Throw out the trash. Secure the areas used by the after-school program before leaving.

TIP 37

Learn to Deal with
Conflict and Criticism

"Just as surely as some people bring out your best and others bring out your worst, you can be one of the few who brings out the best in others at their worst. It's a matter of stabilizing yourself when dealing with them, understanding the positive intent behind their bad behavior, identifying a direction and organizing your own behavior around that direction."
— *Brinkman and Kirschner, in* Dealing with Difficult People

No matter how much you may want to avoid it, principals and after-school program directors frequently find themselves involved in or expected to mediate conflict situations. It is an unavoidable part of the job.

Together, take a class or workshop in conflict resolution. Learn how to manage conflicts to minimize risks, maximize benefits and increase personal and professional growth. Know yourself and your conflict resolution style. Are you an avoider, an accommodator, a compromiser, a competitor or a negotiator? How about your partner?

Additionally, teachers in after-school programs must learn that they can't avoid or do away with conflict. They must learn to handle and defuse it in ways that produce growth and constructive solutions. They must acknowledge others' feelings. Help them learn to treat others with respect, listen, focus on issues rather than emotions or people and use 'I' statements that diffuse the energy of the situation and help express feelings. Personal feelings that are allowed to fester during a mediation session will only re-emerge later.

High-maintenance parents often will test your patience — and the relationship between the school and the after-school program. Whenever you or your partner must discipline the child of one of these overly protective parents, expect to receive a call or confrontation. If high-maintenance parents don't get their way, they'll argue, try to intimidate, threaten or do whatever it takes to get satisfaction.

Don't allow conflict to develop between you and your partner. If you become aware of any incident that the other might hear about from an angry parent, a staff member, a partner or a community constituent, immediately inform the other. Never go home for the night without providing the other with a heads-up notice about a potential complaint or conflict situation. Always guard each other's back.

PART IV

TIPS THAT SUPPORT PROGRAM ORGANIZATION

"The productivity of work is not the responsibility of the worker but of the manager."
— Peter F. Drucker

Research from the 1980s on effective schools lists a safe and orderly environment as one of its important correlates. In an effective school, there is an orderly, purposeful, businesslike atmosphere that is free from the threat of physical harm. The school climate is non-oppressive and conducive to teaching and learning. The same must be true for an effective after-school program.

Successful program organization does not exist without planning and attention to the fundamental structures that support efficacy in delivery of services. Leaders of organized programs have no difficulty showing documentation of their work, producing current and accurate records and demonstrating high levels of accountability and results. Their programs are supported with adequate funding, use technologies and continually meet compliance with local, state and national regulatory standards.

When you visit an organized program, expect to find it clean and free of clutter. Children will be observed responding positively to directions from adults. The environment will be welcoming and nurturing. Everywhere, there will be evidence of learning and satisfaction. Adults will be happy and engaged in their work. Everyone will be task-oriented and working to achieve the program vision.

The advice in this section should provide an overview and affirm what you already know about program organization and impart special insights that can help you better organize your work.

TIP 38

Organize an Office

Before your after-school program begins operation, set up an office. For school-based programs, it is essential that the principal designate space for an office. It is also desirable that the space be in a safe, secure, private area in close proximity to the areas of the school used for the after-school program. A small desk in a corner of a busy staff-member lounge lacking any privacy is not conducive to quality work. Worse yet, some after-school program directors have been expected to work from off-campus locations, their cars or even from their homes.

At minimum, the after-school program director's office should include a:

- computer with high-speed Internet and e-mail access;
- laptop and projectors;
- typewriter, copier, fax machine;
- telephone with answering machine;
- cellular phone;
- digital camera and video recorder;
- access to a TV with DVD and VHS player;
- lockable file cabinets with plenty of hanging files;
- electric staplers, pencil sharpeners, etc.;
- calendar;
- safe (for securing important documents); and
- clerical support personnel.

Too many after-school-program directors are expected to complete tasks that should be performed by clerical staff members. Valuable time and efficacy are expended when administrators are forced to complete clerical work for which others are better trained (see Tip 55).

Planning for an office setup takes time and requires an outlay of budgeted funds. Visit other offices or consult with professional interior designers to gain additional ideas about how offices can be arranged to increase efficiency.

Plan
for the Year

Teachers wouldn't enter a classroom without a quality, well-conceived lesson plan. Principals are well-known for their extensive "to-do" lists and planning sessions. Likewise, after-school leaders need to plan, develop schedules, organize their work and conceive projects and commitments in advance. For new leaders, trying to figure out how, what, why, when and where things should be done can be an overwhelming task. It can become discouraging when the work piles up and you fall behind, miss deadlines and allow key opportunities to pass. Experience can help everyone become a better planner, but all after-school leaders can benefit from an outline detailing annual tasks and responsibilities. Add and/or detract from Figure 39a (available at www.schoolagenotes.com) for what needs to be done in your work setting in accordance with your job description.

TIP 40

Conduct

Regular Staff Meetings

It is good practice to hold staff meetings. It is even better to structure meetings so that participants' time is used wisely. An agenda that details time, responsibilities, actions and desired outcomes helps people prepare before the meeting. People can be trained to prepare for meetings, to complete homework and to come to meetings informed and ready to contribute. The manner in which people prepare may differ depending on whether a topic will be discussion only or if a decision will be made. When decisions are made, it is helpful if the facilitator has listed the way that decisions will be reached — affirmation, consensus, vote, etc.

Conducting staff meetings that accomplish the business of the organization in an expedient manner requires the facilitator to have a vision of what an effective meeting should look like after it is completed. The facilitator must plan, prepare and distribute the agenda in advance to inform attendees of expectations. Good meetings also require that minutes are recorded and attention is given to follow-up details relative to the decisions that were made. Get a copy of Robert's Rules of Order to review how to conduct meetings in parliamentary style.

Meetings need to be held at a time and in a place where there are minimal distractions. Keep a record of meeting agendas and minutes. They become historical records of your work. Over time, you might notice trends that indicate agenda items requiring more attention and others needing less. Minutes are helpful to verify and remind people of past discussions and actions.

Figure 40a (available at www.schoolagenotes.com) is a model agenda that can be revised to fit your unique setting.

Manage the Budget;
Balance the Bottom Line

After-school-program directors must learn the procedures for developing an annual budget, completing purchase orders, controlling expenses and acquiring additional revenue streams. This work does not need to remain on the principal's busy plate. Do the work. Keep the principal updated and aware of the bottom line.

After-school program administrators should view their program as a business. Without customers, the business fails. Stay on top of payments due from parents and expenses of payroll, supplies and purchased services. If the program is funded by a grant, the worry about collecting payments from parents is likely reduced. However, funds must be routinely requested from the granting source and expenses managed in a businesslike, professional manner.

Ask questions. Learn how to read a budget spreadsheet and the procedures for reporting expenditures. Spend money in an ethical manner according to the budget guidelines. Authorize purchases and expenditures of funds according to grant or school-district regulations and approved general accounting procedures.

Don't allow mismanagement of funds to derail many other positives of collaboration and compromise the stability of a program that is essential for your children's and their families' welfare.

Be
Accountable

Do what you say you will do. It is unethical to do otherwise. If you tell the principal that you will provide a report by the end of the week, get it done. Excuses and forgetfulness erode the foundation of a collaborative relationship.

Moreover, hold your staff members accountable for their work. Establish goals and work to keep focused on what they must do to achieve them. Report the results as they are. If your efforts fall short, tell the truth. Don't misrepresent the facts to your principal, to the school board or to the community.

Provide those who work in the after-school program what they need to do their jobs. Educators need training and resources to be effective. To provide less than adequate resources and training sets them up for failure. Likewise, report deficiencies in financial or human resources to your superiors who also share responsibility for accountability of your after-school program.

TIP 43

Meet
Compliance Standards

As administrators of after-school programs, it is essential that both leaders are trained and knowledgeable about local and state rules and regulations that must be followed so that your program meets compliance for licensure and regulatory standards. State departments of education and human resources share legal responsibility for establishing minimum standards, training administrators and inspecting sites to ensure that all compliance standards are met. Work to ensure that your program is never cited with a serious risk for children or a rules infraction.

Rules, regulations and processes for ensuring compliance vary by state. For a helpful guide, review the *NAA Standards for Quality School-Age Care* as you work to establish a program or prepare for a site review. The document details the standards for practice in:
- human relationships;
- indoor environment;
- outdoor environment;
- program activities;
- safety, health and nutrition; and
- program administration.

If your program is funded by a grant, you likely will have additional regulatory requirements that must be met and maintained to receive continued funding. Attend conferences and workshops and stay informed about what you must be able to do. Ask questions. Work with a colleague who has experience and success meeting compliance.

TIP 44

Embrace
Technologies

Whether to use technology is no longer an option in education. A capacity to demonstrate technology skills should be a part of every job description. You cannot be an effective leader of an after-school program if you have inferior skills, especially those involving computers and software programs that are essential for doing your job.

At the most basic performance levels, you must be able to:

- create, save, edit, file and retrieve documents using a word-processing program;
- create and use a data spreadsheet;
- create and edit desktop publishing documents and PowerPoint presentations;
- use e-mail (retrieve and add attachments, create distribution lists, maintain contact lists);
- operate a copier and be able to troubleshoot minor technical problems;
- operate a fax machine;
- use multiple features of a cellular phone, digital camera or camcorder;
- tape messages for your office phone;
- take pictures with a digital camera and upload them to a computer;
- troubleshoot computer and printer errors;
- load and operate computer programs for children;
- use overhead projectors, whiteboards and laptops connected to LCD projectors;
- use personal technology for digital data management; and
- create and maintain a Web site.

If you don't have experience and competence using each of the above, you must be reliant on others to help do your work. Enroll in classes. Hire a personal tutor. Stay ahead of others in your field.

Your after-school program staff members also must have access to technologies and know how to use them. Provide key staff members with cell phones or walkie-talkies to facilitate communication within the center and support security practices. Teach your staff members how to use emerging technologies. Integrate technology into the curriculum, align it with student learning goals and use it for engaged learning projects. Teacher quality is the factor that contributes to and influences student access and learning with technology. Assure that teachers use technology effectively. Use technology to work smarter, not harder.

TIP 45

Write
Grants

Many after-school programs receive a majority of their financial resources and money for day-to-day operations from grants. Grants often have strings attached, restrictions on how money may be spent and limitations on their length. Whether you view grants as a blessing or more trouble than they are worth, money from grants is a major funding source for after-school programming.

There are many entrepreneurs who have developed a career for themselves by writing grants (for a fee) for school districts and community organizations. That might be an option for your program. However, determine whether an outside contractor is allowed to write the grants you may be considering and weigh the pros and cons of paying someone to do work that you or others in your organization may be able to do.

Connect with your state department of education, the state human-services department, and city, county and parish governments for information about grants. There are numerous local, state and federal philanthropic foundations that provide grants for after-school programming and related activities.

When searching for federal education grants, review the following Web sites:

- www.grants.gov — a source to find and apply for federal government grants managed by the U.S. Department of Health and Human Services;
- www.hud.gov/grants/index.cfm — for community groups, U. S. Department of Housing and Urban Development; and
- www.schoolgrants.org — clearinghouse for PreK-12 education grants.

There are numerous list-serves that provide updates of grants and send information about current requests for proposals to which you can subscribe. Review the Web-based resources listed at the end of this book.

Plan ahead when writing grants. Don't wait until the deadline approaches to start your work. Be sure your school or organization meets the criteria to apply. Follow all of the guidelines in the request for proposal. Proofread. Have others read your drafts and provide you with feedback.

The grant-writing processes are most effective when others are involved and share some of the work. That way, when an award is made, there is buy-in for the idea, awareness of what is to be implemented and knowledge of intended outcomes. Grant writing is hard work. Grant implementation works best when it is done with people; it is often a challenge when it is done to people.

PART V

TIPS THAT ASSURE QUALITY PROGRAM DEVELOPMENT

Principals should not support or tolerate after-school programs that do not adhere to standards of quality. Children should not be subjected to sub-par or unsafe environments that lack connections with the regular school day or an ineffective focus on concepts and activities addressed in state standards.

Quality after-school programs provide children with ideal settings to extend their learning day. Quality programs contain components that allow students time to explore, to play and to catch up in areas where learning gaps are evident. They provide time for extended reading and math activities, exploration of the arts, fitness, social development, community service, family engagement and mentoring.

After-school programs do not have the same accountability requirements as schools. After-school programs do, however, support what happens during the school day and provide coherence to what children experience and learn in the regular school day.

Everyone has a role in developing a quality after-school program. Foremost should be the students and parents who choose to participate in them. Their needs should drive decision-making. Tutoring, enrichment, homework help, recreational and social activities should be provided through a continuum of services that meet each child's needs.

Principals and after-school program directors play key roles in assuring that quality content is planned, provided and evaluated. Through effective collaboration, after-school program directors assume many responsibilities related to developing quality content, alleviating an already busy principal of many tasks. But both must actively envision and plan the connections between their entities and engage others in academic planning meetings that further shape the quality of program content.

Review the standards. Embrace them. Attain them. Be creative. After-school programs should provide seamless learning experiences for all children.

TIP 46

Achieve the Standards

The National Association of Elementary School Principals and the National Afterschool Association have published standards for after-school programming. They provide a vision of quality programming and effective performance for those who work in after-school programs. Standards should be challenging but attainable. The standards reflect what is being achieved in thousands of programs and by most leaders, but it is also likely that not every standard is fully achieved by everyone. The standards reflect goals established by peers in the profession that have figured prominently in the development of after-school programming throughout the nation.

Principals and after-school program directors should have copies of both documents. Take a fresh look at your personal leadership abilities and your efforts to share responsibilities of directing after-school programming. Devote a portion of your collaborative meetings to their review and ask yourselves:

- Do we share a common vision of quality after-school programming and do we make that clear to others?
- Is the after-school program fully integrated into the overall school curriculum and extend learning opportunities for children?
- Are there effective systems of communication and processes in place for sharing space and resources?
- Is the after-school program managed effectively so that it operates smoothly and with adequate resources?
- Does the content of the program reflect quality and meet the individual learning needs of students?
- What skills or knowledge do I possess, or need to acquire, that will help me (us) attain the standards?
- What community resources do we use to achieve the standards and what others can we seek out?

- Does the after-school program create stronger links, involvement and support services for families?
- Do the principal and the after-school program director draw upon each other's strengths, share a relationship based on mutual respect and work together to share success of the program with constituents?
- Is there an effective collection and analysis of data of program impact used for evaluation?

NAESP's *Leading After-School Communities* (2006) identifies six standards for what principals should know and be able to do. They are:
- expand the vision of learning;
- act as a community catalyst;
- collaborate to manage resources;
- ensure quality content;
- evaluate after-school programs; and
- champion after-school programs.

The National Afterschool Association's *Standards for Quality School-Age Care* (1997) identifies six standards for children and youth between the ages of 5 and 14. In the first five categories, twenty observable keys of quality are listed. For the administration standard, there are sixteen keys that describe program organization, procedures and policies. The six standards are:
- Human Relationships;
- Indoor Environment;
- Outdoor Environment;
- Activities;
- Safety, Health & Nutrition; and
- Administration.

To learn more, visit these Web sites:
- The National Association of Elementary School Principals — www.naesp.org
- The National Afterschool Association — www.naaweb.org

TIP 47

Develop a
Schedule

Some after-school program directors feel they have too much to do each day and too little time to do it. The truth is, to address each academic component and standard of after-school programming does require a considerable amount of time. The challenge is to develop a schedule that uses time and human resources wisely and assures that students' learning needs are met each day.

The key to an effective schedule is the development of good structure. Organization of time and people is an important task for the after-school program director. Once the plan is developed, it must be communicated to adults in an effective manner and monitored for results.

Each day after school, students should enjoy some planned recreation activities and a healthy snack. Devote time while the snack is served to teaching nutrition tips and addressing manners and social skills. Where programs are well structured, every minute is planned to focus on one or more learning objectives. Where programs are well structured and planned, and adults engage students in effective ways, student management and behavior are seldom serious issues.

Student-to-adult ratios and physical space may limit ways that children can be grouped for instruction. The use of community volunteers and the allowance of time for them to engage in mentoring activities also must be factored into an effective, flexible schedule.

Students' ages should determine how much time is needed for homework completion. A schedule that allows flexibility and independence will help kids stay on task. Students should be grouped so they can experience reading, math and science remediation or enrichment. They also should take part in the development of their daily schedule so they can play, explore new topics and choose activities of their interest.

Figure 47A (available at www.schoolagenotes.com) may be helpful when developing the daily schedule to assure that all program components are addressed.

Evaluate the
Program

Before the program opens, both leaders should determine the indicators that will demonstrate progress, plan the assessment process and reach agreement about intended outcomes. Employ the services of an independent evaluator who is experienced in after-school program management and organization — a professional who has a record of effective practice. Then, develop a plan that documents, measures or assesses program processes and implementation. Such indicators might include:

- hours of daily program operation and length of program duration;
- numbers of students served and attendance;
- frequency and quality of staff-member training and retention of staff members; and
- systems for collecting and managing specific data.

Use qualitative and quantitative data to demonstrate program growth. Determine some indicators of progress that can measure the specific objectives covered in the after-school program. Many other measures of student progress will involve and reflect the cumulative work of the student in regular school as well as after school. Ultimately, the No Child Left Behind Act influences the way schools are held accountable for student achievement. Likewise, after-school programs must be able to demonstrate a positive impact on students' reading and math performance. Smart principals and after-school program directors share the vision of how extended learning opportunities can create positive results and collaborate to make it happen.

Develop ways to measure student social growth, behavior, attitude, motivation and self-responsibility. Set realistic goals for assessing parental involvement and the effectiveness of services provided for families.

When evaluating your program, ask:

- Did we do what we said we were going to do?
- How well did we do it?
- What can we do to make it even better?

TIP 49

Evaluate with Numbers, Stories

Numbers are a necessary and an integral part of quantitative evaluations. Standards are typically based upon quantitative measures. However, stories are also very powerful and the soul of qualitative measures. Be sure to collect data that can be used to evaluate the quantity of your program outcomes and the quality.

Often, appreciative parents will tell you in their own words how much the after-school program means to them. Accept their compliments with gratitude, then write down what was said. Ask the parent if you can use their testimonial as part of the program evaluation. If confidentiality issues are addressed and assurances made about how the qualitative data will be used, most parents will gladly allow their comments to be used — and they'll likely share more.

Ask the children how they feel about their participation and learning experience in the after-school program. Seek feedback from volunteers and community partners. Structured interviews and surveys are common means to obtain such data, but listen, remain open and document unsolicited feedback and testimonials.

Potential funders and policymakers will review the numbers and facts that demonstrate progress. But statistics can be manipulated and skewed. And sometimes, numbers simply don't record and capture the true picture. Collect stories. Tell them with passion. People will more likely remember what you say, and gain a clearer sense of program progress and outcomes, by the qualitative data you present instead of the cold, hard facts.

Numbers play to the mind, stories to the heart. Your program wins when you positively influence people's hearts and minds.

TIP 50

Develop a
Transportation Plan

For after-school programs in urban areas, transportation is likely to be less of an issue than in rural areas. Regardless, you must develop a plan for how each student gets home or is picked up from your program. Get to know your families and their needs and be able to structure your program to fit unique circumstances. In some situations, quality content is delivered on buses while students are transported to or from after-school program sites.

The principal and the after-school program director should consider transportation issues while the program is being conceived and developed. Even in urban areas, the safety of children and parents on streets after dark must be factored into transportation decisions.

When developing a transportation plan, the principal and after-school program director should answer the following questions:

- How many students would take advantage of transportation if it was provided?
- What percentage of the budget is realistic to devote toward transportation costs?
- Should enrollment costs vary to accommodate transportation needs?
- What source of transportation is available? (School district buses, public transportation, private contractors, etc.)
- Can any transportation costs be reimbursed from other funding sources?
- What regulatory guidelines must be followed when developing a transportation plan?
- Should late-pick up fees be assessed for tardy parents, and if so, by how much?

- What information will be shared with parents in advance about procedures in the event that a child is not picked up within a reasonable amount of time?
- What source of transportation is available for field trips?
- What procedures must be followed to secure a bus and who has authority to request one?
- Who assumes responsibility for discipline issues that occur on buses while students are enrolled in the after-school program?

These questions do not encompass all issues that should be considered in your setting. They are intended to be a starting point and guide the principal and after-school program director in collaborative planning.

PART VI

TIPS THAT SUPPORT DEVELOPMENT OF PROGRAM INFRASTRUCTURE

An effective after-school program is realized when leaders have a clear vision and empower others to embrace and share it. Then, once the vision is clarified, leaders focus on building a solid infrastructure that continually supports it.

Much has been written about after-school program quality. Read and become familiar with it, but understand the primary importance of a clear vision and the secondary need to build the infrastructure. Perhaps just as important as the development of the infrastructure, and in a broad sense the most fundamental activity of infrastructure, is the development of an effective collaborative relationship and partnership. If either is weak, program quality, organization and other objectives will suffer.

The tips in this section are presented to point out some key aspects of infrastructure that without clarity and constant attention will place an after-school program at risk.

TIP 51

Focus on **Cleanliness**

Cleanliness is a great virtue. Keep your after-school programs clean. Make sure that all staff members understand the requirements for sanitation and work continually to meet high standards. If you move something, put it back. If you make a mess, clean it up.

A bigger issue with cleanliness in after-school programs involves the ineffective relationship with custodians. Where expectations and directives from the principal are clear, and the after-school program director and staff members establish working relationships with custodians, complaints are minimal — and program areas are kept clean. Where those relationships are not developed, conflicts dominate valuable time and can derail programs. The development of close relationships with key workers is the key to keeping centers clean. Relationships are key to effective after-school programming.

Teach children to show pride in their program area. Pick up paper, clean up spills, dust regularly, throw away trash and clean toys and games regularly. Wipe down windows and door handles and other areas where contact with germs can spread communicable disease.

Maintaining cleanliness is not the sole responsibility of the principal. Meet regularly and walk through the after-school program area. Talk about what you observe. Share your expectations with students, staff members and parents.

And don't forget to include the custodians in conversations that pertain to cleaning.

Hire the
Best People

It is not easy to locate, recruit, interview and hire good workers. Those who invest the time, energy and resources will reap the benefits.

Principals have great influence in their communities and awareness of information about substitute teachers, college education majors, retired teachers and individuals with experience for classified and support positions. They also have experience interviewing and negotiating the processes for hiring.

Hiring personnel for the after-school program should be the most-perfected collaborative activity for principals and after-school program directors. It is also one for which both must reach agreement regarding processes and decision-making. It is also imperative that principals play a key role in determining what staff members work in their schools.

In communities where the job market is saturated with prospective teachers and other support-staff members, after-school programs can be a training ground for new teachers. After-school programs also provide an opportunity for practicing teachers to extend their services and increase earnings. They provide a means for retirees to continue contributing to the profession.

But no matter where candidates come from, developing processes for finding and selecting staff members for after-school programs is important. Devote sufficient time to planning and doing it right.

TIP 53

Provide
Ongoing Training

Principals know the value of staff-member development training. Likewise, after-school program directors must provide training for their staff members. Professional-development offerings should be above and beyond what is minimally required for credentials or child-care regulatory requirements. To advance the field of after-school education, staff members at all levels must be highly trained.

Take advantage of local, state and national professional-development offerings. Your state and national professional associations offer many training opportunities, many of which are free or have minimal costs. Encourage staff members to engage in online learning courses. Create study groups at work. Use this book as a reflective guide for the development of effective collaborative practices.

Lead by example. Engage in continual learning experiences for yourself and make sure your staff members know about them.

TIP 54

Identify

Solutions, Not Problems

Unfortunately, in many work sites the culture is unhealthy and negative. Complaining is the norm. Where frustrations are not addressed, tensions rise and people personalize their issues. Conflicts escalate. People become adept at identifying problems, even celebrating them, but not at solving them. It takes a special leader to turn that culture around. A wise leader sets a positive tone.

Listen when people bring issues and problems to you, but train them also to bring solutions. Promote brainstorming and guard against dismissing the bright ideas that others present.

Some may view this tip to be somewhat controversial. Without a doubt, there will be numerous circumstances where solutions may be very challenging and even inappropriate for lower level staff members to recommend or try. In those cases, the principal and after-school program director must be informed and step in. However, where workers are empowered to solve their own job-imbedded problems, think of ways to work more efficiently and assume responsibility, work quality and self-satisfaction are higher.

An environment where employees can discuss problems and concerns is healthy. But an infrastructure and culture that allows the identification of problems without encouraging suggested solutions is unhealthy.

TIP 55

Invest in
Clerical Support

Let's face it. There are people who can effectively lead and others who contribute better behind the scenes. Don't make the mistake of trying to lead your after-school program and complete all the clerical tasks associated with it. Budget the time and funds for clerical support. Highly qualified and efficient workers will provide the support that will enhance accountability and provide the glue for most of your program infrastructure.

Your clerical staff members will perform many essential duties: typing, bookkeeping, recordkeeping, attendance, file management, budget/fiscal management, computer/data entry and office-machine management, to name a few. Treat them well, pay them a fair market wage and allow them to contribute to the development of an effective program.

TIP 56

Don't Overlook
the Details

The little things make a big difference. Together, the little things are the building blocks that support larger structures. Each one fits with others to create a solid infrastructure. Otherwise, the structure eventually will topple.

What are some of the little things? Where do people drop the ball?

- If you say you're going to do something, follow through and do it.
- Teach your staff members to perform random acts of kindness.
- Make sure that all staff member files are complete and that all student files are complete, signed by parents and filed in an appropriate, organized manner.
- Keep efficient records.
- Be prompt. Adhere to your schedule.
- Don't procrastinate. Deal with minor issues before they become major problems.
- Teach children the guidelines necessary for effective management (that is: how to make lines, the difference between inside and outside voices, how to maintain personal space, how to enter a room in a quiet manner, how to interact with adults, manners, how to play, how to make friends, etc.).
- Honor the time commitments of your collaborative partner. Do little things to help lighten each other's workload.
- Smile while you work.

TIP 57

Offer
Classes for Parents

The development of an after-school program infrastructure must consider family needs. Efforts to raise a child up, especially out of poverty, will be thwarted unless the family is provided assistance, especially the parents. Partner with community agencies to provide parent classes, especially GED, at the after-school program while the children are there and at other times convenient for working parents.

Train a staff member in the use of the Benefit Bank (http://www.thebenefitbank.com/). This Web-based program can help low and moderate income families apply for state and federal benefits. Many families miss out on various forms of support because they lack knowledge, awareness and skills to seek out assistance for which they qualify.

Work with parents to identify their needs. High school graduates might benefit from mock-interviewing classes, help with completing job applications, parenting classes, computer classes or reading and math support.

When children see their parents engaged in learning activities, they are shown a very positive role model. Adults and children learning together will enhance the quality of the after-school program — and greatly reduce student-management issues. Help adults strengthen their educational levels. It will increase their employability and income — immeasurable gifts from an after-school program.

Encourage Links with

Preschools and Head Start

When a child moves on from preschool, many working parents are in need of and search for quality before- and after-school care. Where partnerships exist, a smooth transition for children can be developed. One of the best and most logical partnerships that can be developed by after-school program leaders is with area preschools and Head Start programs. Resources, especially human resources and training opportunities, also can be shared that support the infrastructure of both programs.

Many preschools and Head Start programs operate as non-profit organizations. Leaders of those programs should be consulted for ideas and advice regarding after-school program sustainability.

Effective after-school program directors list the leaders of other non-profit organizations among their closest colleagues and partners.

Seek Labor Support from
Department of Human Services

Many after-school program budgets are stretched to pay the minimal amount of staff-member salaries necessary to remain within regulatory adult-child ratios. What if you could get free workers? How helpful would it be to have a custodial assistant, an office helper, a reception-ist, help with tutoring or assistance with your food-service operations? Investigate the opportunities that exist within your community. Support your program's infrastructure and gain the benefits of extra hands by developing partnerships with the local department of job and family ser-vices and become a host placement site for the work experience program (WEP) and similar programs.

These partnerships require patience and understanding of adult learning styles — similar skills your staff members should possess to be able to effectively work with children. Parents of children enrolled in your program also may qualify for this type of public assistance and the collaborative partnership can be beneficial in numerous ways.

For school-based programs, check school procedures and negotiated agreements with the principal when considering this partnership. Ensure that workers have completed background checks and meet requirements for employment at the standard of paid staff members.

Demonstrate
Sustainability

For after-school programs funded by grants with limited duration, sustainability is an issue that must be addressed early on. Many school districts do not have sufficient or extra resources that can be promised and committed for long-term sustainability of after-school programs. It is not that administrators and decision-makers don't value after-school programs — they simply lack discretionary funds for any extras.

The after-school program director must think like an entrepreneur. Operate the program like a business. Establish the after-school program with nonprofit status and structure the program so that it is governed from outside, but in partnership with, the school district. This type of structure allows for the development of a fee-structure as well as a free, scholarship admission for students and families. It also provides the entrepreneur the freedom to apply for other grants, develop revenue streams that are unavailable to the school district, establish partnerships that generate funds and create a funding system that can operate outside the bureaucracy of the school district.

Why is this an issue of infrastructure and collaboration? If you don't plan, and encompass sustainability in every part of building the infrastructure, the program will remain at risk of financial stress and ruin. Developing a sustainability plan is much easier — and more likely to work — when it is envisioned and developed by two or more people, rather than one person in isolation.

Sustainability requires imagination, capacity to do business as a business and hard work. It may be foreboding, but it can be done if you think like a businessperson. There are many nonprofit organizations that, with time, have created effective sustainability plans. Study them. Ask questions. Take risks. Work hard. Learn how to make money and learn how to make money work for you.

TIP 61

Create an Advisory Committee

Advisory committees can be helpful in broadening support for after-school programs. They advise, they do not govern. Governing boards serve other purposes, especially for nonprofit organizations. Advisory committees help plan programs, serve as a sounding board and provide the eyes and ears of the community.

Advisory committees typically consist of:
- parents;
- teachers;
- school district personnel and central office staff members;
- after-school program staff members;
- business leaders;
- school board members;
- higher education representatives;
- city or town council members;
- community partners; and
- health and social-service representatives.

In some cases, students have successfully participated on advisory committees.

An advisory committee should meet at minimum four times each year. This ensures that the collaboration stays focused on results and accountabilities. Members advise on issues including, but not limited to:
- curriculum;
- quality instruction;
- family activities and services;
- student services;
- needs assessments;
- resource development;

- data analysis;
- continuous improvement planning;
- staff-member collaboration;
- links between school and after-school programs;
- program climate; and
- clarification of program vision.

It is helpful to provide prospective advisory team members with a description of the parameters of duties they are asked to perform, times of meetings and to include them in selecting other members.

Why discuss this as part of the infrastructure? Developing effective after-school programs requires two-way communication, active involvement and ownership from the community. Create an advisory team, or some other type of group that allows constituents to share their views, as part of your collaboration efforts to develop a solid program infrastructure.

TIP 62

Prepare for
Departures; Train Others

Hire good people, but plan for their departure. Everyone can be replaced if you plan and prepare for separations. The principal and the after-school program director should maintain resumes and files of those who express interest in potential job openings. They should work together to fill openings.

Contracts should be developed that specify a time period for submitting resignations. For key positions in after-school programs, several weeks' notice allows time for posting a vacancy, interviewing and hiring an individual. In most cases, it will be advantageous for the new hire to work with the departing employee during a period of transition.

Effective leaders quietly prepare for their eventual departure by training and grooming their replacement (see Tip 88).

Why should you care? If you are promoted to a position of increased authority and compensation, why should you worry about your successor? Because effective leaders plan for transitions and work to ensure that what they develop can be sustained by others.

PART VII

TIPS THAT DEVELOP ADVOCACY FOR AFTER-SCHOOL PROGRAMMING

Principals and after-school program directors are busy people. Both have numerous daily supervisory duties, make countless decisions and engage in many leadership activities centered on clarifying expectations, vision and mission. But amid the array of activities and responsibilities, don't neglect the importance of advocacy for after-school programming. After all, you are one of the experts, the leader in the ranks with huge amounts of credibility with policymakers and stakeholders. Let them know how important after-school programming is for kids and the need for opportunities for all children. This area of your collaboration requires sincerity and intention to help everyone — not just satisfying your own needs and issues.

Plan regular advocacy activities. The tips in this section are provided to get you started. Advocates never rest. Tell your story and express your needs. Work to gain benefits for all kids.

TIP 63

Share Your Program With Community Leaders

"Policymakers, as well as principals, must focus on a continuum of teaching and learning for children. After-school programs provide a wonderful opportunity to expand a variety of enrichment opportunities — not just academics — beyond the school day."

— *from the call to action,* Leading After-school Communities: What Principals Should Know and Be Able to Do, *NAESP (2006).*

Principals know the challenges of trying to fit everything children must know and be able to do into the limited number of hours of a typical school day and year. Those seeking to create more time have recognized that a child's prime learning doesn't necessarily occur between the morning and afternoon bells. They have re-imagined the time and places that kids can learn — out of school — and the support that their schools receive from an after-school program. The wisest seize every opportunity to invite politicians and community leaders to observe the impact that after-school programs have on kids' social development and academic achievement. Together, effective principals and after-school program directors plan opportunities to showcase for their whole community a new way and time for learning — after school.

Principals and after-school program directors are the experts. Share the stories you see unfolding before you each day. Allow key policymakers to observe and learn firsthand how the educational gaps between the haves and have-nots can be reduced in after-school programs. Work to inform your community leaders about how their investments in after-school education are wise preventative actions and a potential savings of money targeted on ineffective intervention programs.

TIP 64

Join Professional
Networks, Associations

The National Network of Statewide Afterschool Networks, funded by the C.S. Mott Foundation, supports the efforts of 38 statewide networks to build partnerships and policies that are committed to the development and sustainability of quality after-school programs. If your state doesn't have a network, consider what you can do to help organize one. A listing of the statewide networks can be found at: http://www.statewideafter-schoolnetworks.net/about_national_network/index.html.

Get involved. Follow the links to your state's Web site for information about upcoming meetings and activities. Everyone's voice is important for continued advocacy and policy work. Volunteer. People working together assure that their voices are heard and make a difference.

After-school networks are structured so that all constituents are welcome at meetings. Principals and after-school program directors should attend these meetings.

Principals and after-school program directors also need to be connected with their colleagues. If you are not now a member, one of the first things you should do upon putting down this book is to join your state and national professional associations (see the Web resources section of this book). After you've joined, get involved.

You can do that by reading the professional journals and updates that are provided to the membership. Attend workshops and conferences, volunteer to serve on committees, keep up to date by visiting the Web site for current information and vote for your peers who choose to serve in leadership roles. Professional associations for principals and after-school program directors are membership based. The benefits you need are membership driven. Be a good member — let your leaders know what you need to better perform your job. Support your state and national associations by regularly paying your dues and enjoy the numerous benefits that will be yours. If you ignore this tip, you likely will feel alone, isolated and disconnected, and risk becoming a liability to your colleagues and your employer.

The National Association of Elementary School Principals (http://www.naesp.org) and the National AfterSchool Association (http://naaweb.org) are beginning an era of collaborative work. Already, workshops are available that support principal and after-school program director collaboration.

Unlimited opportunities exist in this new era of collaboration and partnership to develop combined learning experiences for educational leaders. Help steer our professional associations to develop initiatives that will support professional development of principals and after-school program directors as we learn to work together. Our important collaboration makes a strong statement to the education community about the vital need and value of extending learning experiences for all American children.

Learning never stops for children. Model continuous learning for adults. Involvement in your state and national associations offers the best arena for opportunities to learn what you need to know to be the best in your jobs.

TIP 65

Give
Speeches and Presentations

Faith-based and community-service groups typically seek guest speakers for their meetings and functions. Ask around and make connections so that you can obtain an invitation. Prepare remarks that can be adjusted to fit any requested time for speeches. When possible, accompany your remarks with pictures, videos, brochures or fact sheets so that listeners can visually relate to what you are saying and carry information away from the meeting.

Time and schedules may not always permit the principal and the after-school program director to attend or speak at the same event. It is certainly impressive when both can share a speaking engagement, but either should be prepared to go alone when needed. Make sure those officials who extend invitations are aware that you and your partner can present as a team.

When presenting, consider the audience's familiarity with your topic. What do they want and need to know? What you say and how you say it should vary. You wouldn't present to children, parents or community partners in the same way or for the same length of time.

Tell stories. Share your personal reactions and feelings to what you have encountered in the field. Show enthusiasm. Alter the dynamics of your voice. Make eye contact and connect with your listeners.

Be prepared. Know your data. Quite often your listeners will ask questions when your speech is finished. You should be able to extemporaneously talk about:

- the program vision and mission;
- student enrollment and daily attendance rate;
- examples of student progress and program success;
- vignettes and testimonials that personalize satisfaction;

- the numbers of paid staff members and volunteers working with the program;
- parent engagement activities;
- quality components of after-school programming;
- special program activities;
- community partnerships;
- the school/after-school partnership and shared resources;
- funding needs; and
- volunteer needs.

People are likely not to remember everything you say during a presentation. However, they are very likely to remember what you looked like, the sound and quality of your voice and how you made them feel. Focus on connecting with people. You will gain confidence by practicing and reflecting with your mentor.

The skills and competencies you gain from making presentations are invaluable. Approach every audience with the goal of turning them into advocates for your program. You will increase your realm of influence. When you possess influence, you can persuade others to follow. When people follow, you can lead!

TIP 66

Sign Up for E-mail List-Serves

Stay current with what is happening in the field of after-school programming by signing up for list-serves that distribute news, information, grant ideas, best-practice advice, advocacy tips and updates, new resources and a variety of other important facts and services to help you with your job. Principals and after-school program directors should take advantage of these electronic and free resources. Talk about what you learn. An effective collaborative relationship means that both partners are connected and share.

Check with your state department of education, department of human and child resources, state after-school network, and state and national after-school professional associations for available list-serves. School-Age NOTES, publisher of this book, provides the School-Age Note of the Day, a free service that offers helpful tips and information sent via e-mail Monday through Friday (www.schoolagenotes.com). Keep your e-mail and contact information current.

Don't be left in the dark and miss time-sensitive information that can affect your program. Assume responsibility for staying informed and connected with your colleagues.

TIP 67

Check Association
Web Sites for Alerts and Updates

Principals and after-school program directors can benefit from a wealth of information and resources by visiting their state and national association Web sites. Bookmark the sites. Visit them often for updates. Share what you learn with others.

The National Association of Elementary School Principals has an extensive collection of data and archived articles from survey results related to after-school programming. This information can be helpful when researching the literature for professional growth activities.

State and national professional associations sponsor annual conventions and regional workshops for their members. Plan now to attend one or more functions. If you miss an event, go online and review the conference program to obtain an overview of the current discussion topics and workshops presented by scholars, researchers and your fellow practitioners. Stay current with what is happening in the field.

TIP 68

Develop a Plan for
Public Relations

*"There is only one thing in the world worse than being talked about,
and that is not being talked about."*
— Oscar Wilde

The after-school program director must develop a plan for informing key stakeholders, constituents, parents and school personnel about the program. A good public relations plan creates public awareness, accentuates the program's mission and celebrates the positive accomplishments and outcomes of the program.

Attaining good public relations is an everyday activity. It is the result of form and substance. What you (or others) say about your program and how you (or they) say it will determine what the community will think, know and remember about the success or failure of your after-school program.

An effective public relations plan includes:
- clear objectives, goals and strategies;
- one or more identified targeted audiences;
- a scheduled plan for release of news and information;
- communication vehicles for telling your message; and
- an evaluation of results.

At minimum, routine public relations efforts should involve the production of weekly and/or monthly newsletters. Additionally, your public relations plan should incorporate routine letters to stakeholders, news releases, shared radio, television and newspaper interviews, guest columns or letters to the editor, facility tours and open houses.

Take pictures that promote the activities in your program and use them in your public relations plan. Also, include the stories that led up to the picture, and the events and outcomes that developed afterward.

A public relations plan is based upon effective marketing strategies. If you don't market your program, no one will!

TIP 69

Organize a Rally for
Lights On Afterschool

A project of the Afterschool Alliance, Lights On Afterschool rallies have been organized throughout the nation since 2000 to call attention to the importance of after-school programs. The event draws more than 1 million participants each October. Data shows that 1 in 4 youth, or 14.3 million children, are left alone and unsupervised after school. The purpose of the Afterschool Alliance's annual event is to promote the overarching benefits of after-school programs — safety, help for working families and extended learning — and the need for funding for adequate numbers of programs.

Lights On Afterschool is supported by the After-School All-Stars, Boys & Girls Clubs of America, 4-H Afterschool, Junior Achievement, the 21st Century Community Learning Centers, Young Rembrandts and the YMCA of the USA.

Why are these rallies important and why should you participate and organize an event at your site? Lights on Afterschool is an organized advocacy opportunity. The Afterschool Alliance provides a variety of ideas, training and support materials. It is important that lawmakers and elected officials understand the need for after-school programs within their communities, observe programs in operation, talk with parents, students and staff members, and publicly recognize the positive outcomes.

Events span a continuum from very large and elaborate to small and modest. The point is to invite the community to your program and tell your story. Organize an event and invite your community's:

- mayor;
- city council;
- county commissioners;

- business leaders;
- state legislators;
- federal legislators;
- school board members, central office administration, principals and teachers;
- parents; and
- community partners.

Why should you do this? Because the example of schools and community organizations working together to provide for children and families will resonate well in any community. The public wants to see public schools better used as a community focal point and resource. Showcase what you do. Key leaders can also become passionate about your work and mobilized to exert their influence to help sustain your work.

To learn more about the Afterschool Alliance and Lights on Afterschool, go to www.afterschoolalliance.org.

PART VIII

TIPS THAT SUPPORT PARENT AND COMMUNITY ENGAGEMENT

The success of an after-school program is greatly enhanced by active parental involvement and community engagement. But it takes work and a focused effort to build effective relationships with parents. Your community is rich with resources that can support and sustain your program, but you have to market what you do. Successful parental and community engagement practices are all about marketing.

The tips in this section are provided to prompt ideas for marketing practices that will enhance your after-school program. By creating a program that engages the community, the program will continue to prosper.

Develop a
Recruitment, Enrollment Plan

It is obvious that students need to be enrolled in an after-school program. But which ones? How many? Are there requirements that dictate which ones should be targeted? How will students and their parents be made aware of the program? What happens if demand exceeds allowable space? Worse, what if students don't want to attend?

These and many other questions and issues about enrollment need to be well thought out and planned. Determining the recruitment and enrollment process is an important collaborative activity. The principal needs to play an active role in deciding which students should be invited, especially if the program is funded by 21st CCLC grant funds. The principal is the key link in communicating the referral and selection processes clearly to teachers. The principal also has tremendous influence with parents and can use it to encourage student/family participation. Parents and staff members will surmise the quality of the collaboration between the principal and the after-school program director as this activity is experienced.

The following considerations should be addressed when developing a student recruitment/enrollment plan:

- What are the minimum and maximum enrollment limits for the after-school program?
- At what capacity can the program operate and remain within licensure guidelines?
- Will a waiting list be established? By whom?
- Will a registration fee be assessed?
- Will the program operate with free enrollment or a tuition fee structure?

- Will there be staggered tuition fees assessed if more than one child per family enrolls?
- When are payments due and in what form?
- Will charges be assessed if children are not picked up on time?
- Who will keep the after-school program administrator aware of changes in family information (that is, address change, phone change, qualification status, etc.)?
- What required registration forms must be used?
- If registration forms are incomplete, will a child be allowed to begin participation?
- Will home visits be made to retrieve late registration forms? Who will make the visit?
- Will a student/parent orientation be held? Who will be responsible? Who prepares the student/family handbook?
- What enrollment options will be offered? Full-time or part time?
- Will drop-ins be allowed? What will be provided on late arrival or early dismissal days? What about teacher workshop days (full days when schools are closed)?

Your enrollment form should include agreements with parents about photography and videography of their children, permission for field trips, emergency medical information, consent to provide emergency care, authorization to administer medication, custody arrangements, pickup procedures, second-person authorization and refund practices (if applicable).

Without a doubt, registration can be a very tedious activity. Assign staff members who are efficient, pleasant, patient and welcoming to conduct and oversee this process. Use the time with parents to get to know them, learn about their needs, and explain the mission of your program. As Seth Godin describes in his book, *The Purple Cow,* use this time with customers to create the "wow experience." Parents who are impressed with your service will tell their friends. When that happens, you won't have problems recruiting students to the program.

One-On-One
Engagement Works Best

There is no doubt that children whose parents are involved in what happens at school have greater potential for success than those whose parents show little interest. Initiatives that are designed to engage parents, such as family nights, parent organizations and volunteer activities typically attract those who are inclined to get involved. Often, the most successful programs are found in schools with middle-class, medium-income families. It becomes frustrating for principals and after-school program directors to invest time planning parent programs only to have a handful show up.

Focus more on what you can do, and do it well. Parents must pick up their children from the after-school program. The quality of the adult interactions that occur during that short period can increase levels of respect and trust. Encourage all staff members to fully use that time to connect with parents, build relationships, ask questions, listen and identify needs. It is through those positive one-on-one interactions that strong partnerships are cultivated. Effective, well-attended parent programs are realized when adults work face-to-face to plan and implement them. Principals must recognize the quality of the relationships that are typically built between parents and after-school personnel and encourage and support those activities with their visibility and involvement.

Many parents will appreciate a cup of coffee and an opportunity to review key resources, information and practical tips that can help them manage their busy lives. They also will react well to a smile and a positive remark about their child. Parent engagement is best when it is a daily, intentional activity. Focus efforts on engaging parents and building partnerships that lead to improved student learning outcomes. A one-on-one approach with ongoing conversation builds a strong alliance.

TIP 72

Help Build Bridges Out of Poverty

After-school programs funded by 21stCCLC support the needs of students and families in high-poverty schools. Principals and after-school administrators with responsibilities for these programs must be informed about the research, causes, facts and assumptions that can affect their work with people from poverty. They must also become knowledgeable of communication and instructional strategies that help children of poverty achieve success in middle-class schools and after-school programs.

Dr. Ruby Payne and her associates at aha! Process (www.ahaprocess.com) have a collection of publications that should be part of every professional resource library for anyone who works with children of poverty. aha Process! also provides school and community programs and workshops. Learn as a team. Learn about yourself. Learn about others. Learn how to help others.

Schools exist to help people achieve success in the middle class. For children in poverty, that success can remain elusive until they understand the hidden rules of the middle class. It is just as important that their parents learn the hidden rules. It is even more critical that adults working in an after-school program understand the hidden rules and survival strategies of families in poverty. The keys to building successful relationships are to understand, to teach rules of the middle class, and model behaviors that people must attain for success in school, at work, at home and in the community.

Poverty is the extent to which people or communities do without resources. Children, adults, schools and communities all need resources to succeed. Study and learn about what you can do, the influence you possess and the resources you can provide to aid those in need.

TIP 73

Smile and **Listen**

"Too often we underestimate the power of a touch, a smile, a kind word, a listening ear, an honest compliment, or the smallest act of caring, all of which have the potential to turn a life around."
— *Leo Buscaglia*

You build relationships with people by smiling and listening. How well do you listen? Listening is an attitude, not a skill. Most people have the ability to hear, but not all really listen. When your co-partner is speaking, it is essential that you choose to listen.

No matter what you choose to wear to work each day, don't forget to smile. If you smile, you will:
- be more attractive;
- brighten your mood;
- exercise your facial muscles;
- reduce stress;
- boost your immune system;
- lower your blood pressure;
- make more friends; and
- appear successful.

When leaders smile, they brighten a room, change the moods of others and make people more comfortable. A smiling person spreads happiness. Smile and you will draw people to you.

When you actively listen, it is an effective practice to paraphrase and use your own words to verbalize your understanding of the message. Respond to more than just the meaning of the words you hear and look for the feelings or intent beyond the words. If you don't understand what another person is saying, ask them to repeat or say things in another way. Use eye contact and listening body language.

Active listening is a very effective first response when the other person is angry, hurt or expressing difficult feelings toward you, especially in relationships that are important to you. Be empathic and nonjudgmental. You can be accepting and respectful of others and their feelings and beliefs without invalidating or giving up your own position, or without agreeing with the accuracy and validity of another view.

Practice your smiling and listening techniques. Use them wisely to enhance your communication skills — and the quality of your collaborative partnership.

TIP 74

Develop a
Weekly Bulletin

To engage your community, make sure they learn about your program's vision and mission on a regular basis. Develop a catchy format for a weekly newsletter or informational bulletin and share it with your constituents.

To "go green" and save paper, publish an electronic version of your weekly bulletin. Develop e-mail distribution lists of your constituents and regularly send the newsletter the same day of each week. People will become used to looking for it.

The contents of a weekly bulletin can include:

- summary of activities, special events and accomplishments;
- pictures;
- calendar of upcoming events;
- clarification of expectations;
- advocacy messages;
- highlights of staff members, volunteers, students, partners, parents; and
- warm fuzzies.

Weekly newsletters can be archived on your Web site and used to document activities and progress of your program. A weekly newsletter provides direction and helps people avoid wasting time until they are told what to do. Preparing a calendar of activities will force you to get organized and help others avoid surprises. A weekly bulletin is a form of documentation of your collaborative partnership.

A weekly bulletin will become a valuable marketing tool. Devote the necessary time to developing a quality product.

TIP 75

Respond Promptly to
Phone Calls and E-mails

If your constituents have a need to call or e-mail you, their reason must be important. You will not earn their respect or conduct efficient business if you fail to respond that same day. Show this professional courtesy to everyone, but especially with your collaborative partner.

Discipline yourself to read e-mail regularly throughout the workday. However, don't read your e-mail unless you can devote the amount of time needed to effectively respond to all messages. Delete the junk mail, but don't skip over messages to which you must respond. You will forget them. Your constituents will perceive you to be negligent. The same practice should apply to your phone messages.

Remember, e-mail sent and received from computers in public schools can become a public record. Don't write anything in an e-mail message that you wouldn't want to appear in a court of law. Moreover, if you must address an employee with an unpleasant message, speak to them face to face rather than through e-mail. Don't write or reply to an e-mail message when you are angry.

Train your assistant to screen phone messages and also to inform your constituents about your availability to accept and return calls. You know it is frustrating to be routed to voice mail only to find out later that the person you tried to call was in their office. Busy people waste tremendous amounts of time playing phone tag. To help reduce wasted time, you should:

- place a message on voice mail when you are away from the office stating when you will return;
- instruct your assistant to inform callers when you can accept calls, or the best time and number would be for you to return calls;
- speak slowly and clearly when you speak into the phone;

- prepare what you want to say before you make a call; and
- emphasize your phone number and name by repeating them.

Never leave a sensitive or inappropriate message on an answering machine. You never know who might intercept it.

Set the tone about the importance for positive and punctual communication. Make this a priority in the development of your collaborative partnership.

TIP 76

Get Program Support from Community Partnerships

Take advantage of the wealth of resources in your community that can enhance programming, often at no expense. Principals and after-school program directors must meet, share ideas, identify needs, plan, connect with community agencies and forge partnerships that will provide learning experiences for children and influential community support for the after-school program.

Work as a team to cultivate partnerships that support student learning with representatives of the following:

- United Way;
- 4-H;
- YMCAs;
- health department;
- medical centers;
- schools and universities;
- faith-based organizations;
- government agencies;
- businesses;
- volunteers;
- Big Brothers-Big Sisters;
- vocational/career centers;
- music clubs; and
- parks and recreation departments.

Partnerships with influential individuals from key agencies and community organizations can support program sustainability. Most important, strong community connections create positive learning opportunities for children.

Conduct
Surveys

Even though you might be capable of instinctively perceiving what your parents (or other constituents) think about your after-school program, the data collected from surveys, questionnaires or needs assessments provide a more accurate representation. Good data will help guide decision-making related to program improvement. It can also be used with public relations campaigns.

The most common complaint from those who have conducted surveys is that a large percentage of them are never returned. To change that (and save paper), use technology to get better results. Set up a survey on your Web site (such as shown in Figure 77a, available at www.school-agenotes.com), with links on the computers in your lab and those used by students. As parents arrive to pick up their children, request that they take a couple of minutes to complete the survey. Most will. You'll also discover who is computer-literate and who is not. Most will want to learn — and your parent coordinator can make important connections and create opportunities for valuable parent training and assistance.

PART IX

TIPS THAT SUPPORT PERSONAL CARE

"We expect our leaders to be better than we are ... and they
should be — or why are we following them?"
— *Paul Harvey*

An important component of after-school programming is the development of nurturing activities that advance healthy minds, bodies and souls. It is difficult to get kids to understand those concepts if the program leaders are out of shape and neglect their own personal care.

It is essential that leaders of after-school programs support each other in their continual development of high quality professional and personal lives. It is extremely challenging (and likely impossible) to develop a collaborative relationship with a partner who is physically, emotionally or attitudinally unfit.

Model a positive personal relationship for others, especially the children. Encourage your partner to develop healthful eating habits and engage in regular exercise activities. Look out for others' welfare. Work to reduce stress that can detract from the productivity of your program. Model the good habits described in this section for staff members and students. Set the tone.

Don't Smoke

If you smoke, quit. And if you don't smoke, don't start. If you are old enough to read this book, chances are that you understand the dangers of long-term exposure to smoking and are committed to protecting children from it. We clearly know the dangers. We also know that education is the key to preventing kids from engaging in bad habits, and kids learn best from positive role models. You must be one of those positive role models. But kids are clever and will see through your disguises. They'll notice that you take breaks, vacate the center, sit in your car and puff away.

The physical demands of your work after school will require good health, strength, regular attendance and an ability to work long hours. Smokers are viewed as a health-care liability. Your program's long-term success depends upon your health and your ability to do an effective job. Smoking is one of the worst things you can do to your body.

Need more reasons? What about:

- bad breath;
- yellow teeth;
- smelly clothes;
- more colds and coughs;
- difficulty keeping up with friends when exercising; and
- an empty wallet: Cigarettes and tobacco products are very expensive!

Most regulatory or licensing agencies have made it illegal to smoke in or near an after-school center. Enforce those regulations. Don't be afraid to take a stand and say that smoking is a bad habit. Work to help others kick their bad habit. Teach kids that bad habits can kill them.

TIP 79

Exercise

Principals and after-school program directors who are physically fit are happier, stronger and climb career ladders more quickly than those who are not. They are better prepared to work long hours. They are more attractive to employers because they pose less threat of experiencing heart- or lung-related illnesses. They suffer less from depression.

Invest in a pair of good athletic shoes. Start walking. Walk with your collaborative partner and take advantage of the time to plan while you do. Encourage your staff members and students to walk. Include walking in your daily program schedule. Lead the daily walking activity.

There are many benefits to be gained from walking, such as:

- more energy;
- deeper and more satisfying sleep;
- stronger leg muscles;
- less impact on knees than from running;
- lower body fat;
- higher metabolic rate; and
- reduced stress.

The students that you motivate to become regular walkers will study more effectively and have better recall. Daily physical exercise will also reduce their risk of heart disease, cancer, stroke and high blood pressure, and may even slow the aging process. A program goal would be to engage in 20 to 30 minutes of walking or another form of exercise that raises the heart rate.

Do what works for you, but exercise for your health.

TIP 80

Eat a **Balanced Diet**

Just as with the national campaign to stop smoking, we must learn to reduce our tendencies to carry excessive body weight by eating a balanced diet. It's a simple fact: Eating healthful foods in moderation and engaging in a regular fitness regimen should help you attain and maintain normal body weight.

So why is this tip mentioned in this book? Because you are a leader, and leaders need to set a good example for others.

You will need to serve daily snacks and perhaps even meals during your after-school program hours. To set that good example, those snacks must meet state and federal nutrition guidelines and portion sizes. You must inform your constituents about those standards. Children need daily portions of protein, grains, fruit, vegetables and milk. They need to learn to eat foods from all groups.

School lunches have become a scapegoat and partially blamed for increasing rates of childhood obesity. Without a doubt, if a child would eat excessive amounts of what is served as part of a school lunch, weight gain could become a concern. The reality is, however, that school lunches are balanced and portion sizes controlled according to federal nutritional standards.

Regardless, as the program director, you have direct influence over what is served when kids are under your watch. Set the example. Develop policies about "other" snacks or treats that parents want to share. Stock your vending machines with healthy snacks and beverages. Be creative when planning family activities. Pizza may be cheap, easy and appealing, but it doesn't always convey that your program intends to teach the values of a balanced diet.

The United States Department of Agriculture sponsors MyPyramid. gov, an informative Web site dedicated to good health. It is a resource that after-school program directors should share with their constituents.

TIP 81

Have a
Sense of Humor

"The most wasted of all days is one without laughter."
— *e e cummings*

Is laughter evident in your after-school program? If not, it could be because you, as the program director, have failed to establish a tone that it is okay to laugh, joke, discover and enjoy the funny side of things.

Humor is a universal language. It's contagious and a natural diversion. It brings people together and breaks down barriers. People are attracted to those who have a sense of humor.

Humor is free and has no known negative side effects. Listen to the conversations between children and adults. Listen for laughter. Encourage people to have a good time.

Kids say and do the darnedest things. Enjoy their precious and humorous insights and comments. Write them down. Share them with others. They can be developed into great stories that people will enjoy — and the way they remember your program. Kids' humor can be collected and developed into a book or retirement gift.

Make another person smile! Show your sense of humor.

TIP 82

Maintain a
Positive Attitude

"An attitude is nothing more than a habit of thought."
— *John Maxwell*

We expect children to develop and display a good attitude when enrolled in an after-school program. Yet, sometimes the adults they encounter appear to have little concept of what that means. Kids with bad attitudes are usually reflecting behaviors they have learned from adults.

As the principal or program director, you set the tone each day. Just as you should choose to dress for success, you also choose what kind of attitude to wear to work. And whatever choice you make will be reflected by those around you.

But maybe you are thinking, "As long as I can do the job, what difference does it make what kind of attitude I have?" Simply put, those with a positive attitude are more successful. Attitude is a factor that influences success more than aptitude.

In his book *Attitude 101,* leadership guru John Maxwell offers a chart demonstrating how various attitudes can impact an athletic team of capable players (your staff members, volunteers, students, parents):

Abilities+Attitudes=Result
Great Talent+Rotten Attitudes=Bad Team
Great Talent+Bad Attitudes=Average Team
Great Talent+Average Attitudes=Good Team
Great Talent+Good Attitudes=Great Team

To create and sustain an effective after-school program, you need good, talented people with positive attitudes. As the leader, or coach, results emanate from the attitude you choose to bring to the game.

TIP 83

Develop
Your Charisma

Charismatic leaders know how to work a room. They make those they interact with feel as though they are the most important person in the world. They might possess levels of power and authority, but they gain loyal followers because of their magnetic personality and charm. They are articulate and sensitive to the needs of others. Charismatic leaders exhibit high levels of self-confidence, persistence, determination, passion and optimism.

If you are not naturally charismatic, practice can help develop compelling and appealing skills. Charismatic leaders learn to tell good stories and help people relate to issues by using symbolism and metaphor. They learn how to tug on emotions and use body and verbal language for effect. They take risks and demonstrate elements of self-sacrifice for the organization and their beliefs.

To further your practice and development of charisma, identify opportunities where you can:

- Study tape recordings of speeches and listen for sounds of emotion and nuances of theatrical effects in your voice.
- Study video recordings of your performance while leading others and focus intently on your body language, eye contact, facial expressions and interactions with others.
- Study speeches of charismatic political and religious leaders.

Improvement of charismatic skills can increase your leadership capacity and provide finesse in collaboration processes. But avoid the common pitfall for charismatic leaders — selfishness. If your motivation to increase charisma is for admiration and self-enhancement, you will likely fail in your attempts to lead others.

TIP 84

Reduce Your Stress Levels

Stress is defined as "a mental, emotional, or physical strain caused, e.g. by anxiety or overwork. It may cause such symptoms as raised blood pressure or depression" (Encarta Dictionary, 2008). The principalship is one of the most stressful jobs in a school district. Because of the increasing demands, many individuals choose not to apply for these essential leadership positions. Just like principals, after-school program directors are asked to wear numerous hats and address many demands from constituents in varying situations — all conditions that add to stress.

To cope with those multiple stressors, one must first recognize their effects — emotional, psychological and physical. If you experience headaches, fatigue, irritability, anger, back pain, shortness of breath, eating disorders or more, you are likely experiencing various levels of stress. Without effective management, stress builds and impacts behavior and levels of concentration. Stress can lead to depression and other health problems. Those under stress sometimes turn to smoking, drinking or drugs to alleviate the pressure.

After-school program directors can't change many of the events that cause their stress. But they can learn how to effectively respond to stress and develop patterns of positive behavior that counteract it. To help manage stress, after-school program directors can:

- **Take a break.** When stress builds, get up and take a break. Relax, catch your breath and return to the task at hand with a clearer head.
- **Manage your schedule.** Limit the number of meetings and events you attend that take you away from your primary work responsibilities. You can't be everywhere, so delegate others to attend meetings in your place when appropriate.
- **Get organized.** Many people create stress by failing to organize their office. They can never find anything and waste time re-creating work that should have been placed in files or organized

within the computer. Setting up an efficient office operation can be an important timesaver — and stress reducer. Observe other office operations first before organizing yours if you've never done this before (see Tip 38).

- **Find support.** Every leader needs someone with whom he or she can talk. Even though spouses and friends can be supportive during stressful times, there are times where it is best to reach out to someone outside the realm of the program and school community. Use the resources of your local, regional, state and national associations when looking for support outside your immediate locale (see Tip 92).

- **Don't procrastinate.** When the leader fails to make decisions, the work from subordinates stalls. Procrastination only increases stress.

- **Develop a thick skin.** You'll never make everyone happy all the time. If you do, chances are that levels of change you're advocating are insignificant and you aren't an effective leader. Learn to listen to disgruntled people, but at the same time, learn to move on. Shake off stinging remarks that are meant to hurt you. Call your mentor, reflect and talk through the toughest situations.

After-school personnel can support each other, and the students and parents they serve, by modeling stress reducing behaviors. Together, they can:

- **Relax.** Make it an acceptable and routine practice after school to meditate, practice yoga, enjoy nature and gardening, play with a pet or listen to music.

- **Read.** Talk about the good books you read. Develop book clubs. Teach kids to talk about the books they read.

- **Eat right.** Good nutrition helps reduce tension. Encourage each other to select apples or granola bars instead of doughnuts or candy bars.

- **Get enough sleep.** Sleeping allows your body time to recuperate. Make sure you are giving your body the time it needs to rest.

- **Exercise.** Working out is a great way to relieve stress and stay in shape. Walking is the easiest, and perhaps the best form of daily exercise. Everyone in the after-school program can find time to walk together.

- **Share time with others.** Go to a movie or dinner with friends. Travel. Devote time to your family. Don't allow work to take over your home life and family time.

PART X

TIPS THAT FURTHER PROFESSIONAL DEVELOPMENT

"Learn everything you can, anytime you can, from anyone you can — there will always come a time when you will be grateful you did."
— *Sarah Caldwell*

There is an old adage that two heads are better than one. Brothers Roger and David Johnson (1988), cooperative-learning experts at the University of Minnesota, paraphrase it even better — two heads learn better than one. Where principals and after-school program directors collaborate and intentionally share their professional development activities, they will most assuredly attain a clearer vision for their work, become better leaders, create more solutions to problems, and reap the benefits of higher student achievement and happiness.

The tips and advice shared in this final section of the book can be implemented individually but are better shared together. What one reads should be shared with your partner. When you both read different material and share, each has the potential to learn more. By studying together, sharing professional presentations, becoming effective communicators, and understanding the levels of leadership, your team will become cohesive and strong. Working in isolation, you risk dragging anchor on the other — and on your profession.

TIP 85

Read

After-school programs, especially 21st CCLCs, are structured to help boost student's reading abilities. Therefore, the principal and after-school program director need to model good reading skills and habits.

What do you read? Hopefully, your list includes selections from:

- professional trade books;
- professional journals from state and national associations;
- Web-based list-serve updates;
- newspapers;
- Web sites and other Internet resources;
- children's books;
- leadership books (like this one!); and
- position papers and advocacy materials legal updates.

Readers develop thoughts and opinions that can be shared in conversations and used to influence and effect change. Share good books, professional magazines, articles and Web sites. Never allow yourself to become "too busy" to read.

Set aside time each day to read, just as you do for exercise and eating balanced meals.

TIP 86

Write

Just as important as reading is writing.

As leaders of after-school programs, you must develop skills to effectively write grants, newsletters, contracts, evaluations and numerous other forms of scholarly work. You learn to be a better writer just as you learn to play a piano — with practice.

Get in the habit of writing using a word-processing program. To use a pencil, pen and legal pad will likely show your age. It also means that you perform tasks twice. It is hard to imagine any kind of contemporary professional writing that is not typed or prepared using a computer. Word processing allows you to better see and preview your work, edit while you write and produce a professional looking product. Writing is perhaps the most-important prerequisite skill needed to keep people informed about your after-school program.

Write speeches. The process will help you synthesize information, think through issues and give better presentations. Submit articles to your professional associations and online educators' professional development sites. Write newsletters for your constituents and guest columns for your local newspaper that advocate for after-school programs.

Allow kids to see you write. Be their role model. Talk to them about the importance of writing. Share samples of your work with them and encourage them to "grade" it. They'll love the opportunity to play teacher — and they will also become more motivated to write themselves.

TIP 87

Look
Like a Leader

*"Setting an example is not the main means of influencing
another, it is the only way."*
— *Albert Einstein*

As mentioned in Tip 78, smokers beware. The smoking habit is at an all-time low on the acceptance scale. Smokers are not a protected minority — they are definitely in the minority. Even the smell of smoke on one's clothes can detract from your credibility to lead.

Likewise, other personal characteristics that can count against you are being overweight or slovenly in your professional attire and physical appearance. Principals and after-school program directors who disregard these personal characteristics often unwittingly create concerns about their quality of health. Many people perceive their level of authority and the quality of the program they lead less positively, the least of whom may be the staff members of the school where the program is housed. "But the day-school teachers wear jeans and tennis shoes!" you counter. Regardless, strive to be a leader who looks sharp.

That doesn't mean you have to acquire an expensive wardrobe or wear luxurious jewelry to work. The point is to prepare yourself to look like a professional and assure that you are fit enough to do the job. You are a role model for children. Look the part.

TIP 88

Grow as a **Leader**

"Everyone is a leader because everyone influences someone."
— *John Maxwell, in* Leadership 101

Every principal and after-school program director must learn as much about leadership as they can. Read *Leadership 101* (2002) by John Maxwell for a concise overview of the levels of leadership. The book should be of interest to any leader. Once you can understand the concepts and identify the distinctive behaviors needed at each level of leadership, you can increase your influence and effectiveness with your co-workers.

Maxwell describes the levels of leadership and influence as:
1. position level
2. permission level
3. production level
4. people development level
5. personhood level

Before beginning at the position level, leaders complete their education and earn the right to display a credential. You earn a title with an appointment as a leader and an acknowledged authority and right to be in control. The only real influence at this level is in the job title. Subordinates are concerned about assessing whether you have the capacities to fulfill the job description. People follow because the organizational hierarchy requires them to do so. As Maxwell explains, the leader must display behaviors that demonstrate competency, but not become content to stay at this level. The longer you do, staff moral will be low and turnover high. Unfortunately, too many people never understand the importance of moving above this level.

While preparing themselves for a job, many people form long-lasting interpersonal relationships with others. But a successful growth process hinges on gaining permission from people to form a lasting relationship. Far too many people disregard this concept and fail miserably with their relationships. Yet, in real life, when young people do encounter their significant other, and successfully gain permission, marriage follows. The same type of positive relationship building must begin while demonstrating competencies at position level of leadership. As interrelationships develop, people follow the leader because they want to rather than being obligated to. Work becomes fun. Leaders focus on others' needs and desires. People who are unable to build effective, lasting relationships often find themselves incapable of encouraging others to follow and sustaining their leadership position.

Again, in real life, when couples successfully establish a marriage on a trusting and loving relationship, the results of their commitment often arrive in the form of babies. At the third level of leadership, people come together for a purpose. They like to get together and work to achieve results. Morale is high. People hold each other accountable. They understand and communicate the vision of the organization. The leader focuses on achieving results and attaining quality.

Maxwell cautions leaders about neglecting behaviors needed to support the lower levels of leadership. Followers are always at a different place on the continuum of relationship building, and leaders must maintain awareness of others' needs and the level of influence they share.

As children grow, parents work to help them mature into responsible adults. Leaders at the people-development stage engage in mentoring activities to help others grow and reach their potential. People follow because of what the leader has done for them. Loyalty to the leader is at its highest. Maxwell provides a concise description of the connection between followers and their leaders:

- at level 2, the follower loves the leader;
- at level 3, the follower admires the leader; and
- at level 4, the follower is loyal to the leader.

Many principals are never allowed time to move to the higher levels of leadership. Superintendents often acknowledge their success at the lower levels (1-3) and move them to needier schools where they must begin the process of relationship building and climbing the levels of leadership anew.

It takes longer at each level to move to a higher rank, yet it becomes easier to lead at the upper positions. At the fifth level, leaders are typically at the pinnacle of their careers.

People follow leaders who have attained the personhood level because of who the leader is and what the leader represents to the organization. Leaders at this level work to groom their successor. A smooth transition takes place when a leader of personhood status retires. Principals who attain personhood are sought as consultants, have schools named in their honor or receive other honors.

The higher an individual moves up through the leadership positions, the more the leader grows. It is essential to have an outline. Effective leaders understand the types of behaviors they must exhibit with their co-workers. They understand the need to move between levels and to build and shore up relationships with all employees.

Not everyone will become a great leader, but most can get better by understanding the importance of relationships and working to develop them.

TIP 89

Learn
Together

Individuals who are engaged in collaborative relationships enjoy learning together. When it is appropriate, they attend workshops and conferences as a team. When that is not feasible, one partner attends, learns and collects information to share later with the other.

As collaborators and teammates, principals and after-school program directors create a quality after-school program by:

- advising each other by gathering and reporting information;
- planning together at least once each week;
- collecting, sharing and discussing professional articles and books;
- creating and experimenting with ideas;
- promoting the after-school concept by exploring and presenting opportunities;
- developing, assessing and testing the applicability of new approaches — together;
- organizing and implementing ways of making things work;
- inspecting, monitoring and structuring the infrastructure of the program;
- maintaining and upholding standards and processes;
- teaching each other how to maximize technology;
- presenting together;
- linking, coordinating and integrating the after-school program with the regular school day;
- producing and delivering outcomes; and
- becoming each other's best critical friend.

Learning the intricacies of linking the school day and after-school program is a shared responsibility. The principal and after-school program director must focus their shared learning on this important work. Together, they must assure that their staff members are fully informed of new ideas, procedures and expectations. Communication is the essential process that links people.

TIP 90

Avoid the **Status Quo Syndrome**

*"Progress always involves risks. You can't steal second base
and keep your foot on first."*
— *Fredrick B. Wilcox*

It seems that it becomes more challenging to stay fresh, try new ideas, sustain your passion and change with the times the longer you work at one job or as you become more experienced. Too many educators appear to reach a plateau where they stop growing, lose interest in continuous improvement, and start counting the days to retirement. They become satisfied with the status quo. They do what they have to do to get by and resist any ideas that would change the ways things currently are done.

You can choose to do the same thing day after day and year after year, or you can grow and welcome change. You can look for new challenges and act on them or you can choose to do what you've always done, avoid risks and regress to a state of mediocrity. The sustainability of after-school programs with status quo leaders is doubtful.

Status quo thinkers have difficulty articulating a clear vision of a better future. They fear what might happen. They choose to remain in their own comfort zone rather than changing to do more for the welfare of children. Avoidance of the status quo syndrome requires self-reflection, a willingness to seek honest feedback from colleagues, an awareness of successful progressive practices, self-initiative, motivation to learn and a desire to lead.

TIP 91

Make Sure That
Your Work Is Evaluated

Sometimes, the after-school program director is not provided with an annual performance review. Negotiated agreements might outline the evaluation process, but because after-school program director positions are relatively new in many schools, an evaluation process or form might not exist. The position might not be included in any bargaining unit.

Insist that a process and an evaluation form are developed for your job and that your superior completes it. Don't use the forms or processes used to evaluate school staff members. Your evaluation should be different from other administrators, reflect your abilities to fulfill the job description and be structured in ways that promote growth and development.

In a school-based program, the principal might be assigned as the evaluator, even though the after-school program director collaborates and shares responsibility with the principal. In that case, the after-school program director works at the mercy of the principal — and the success or failure of the partnership and program should be reflected in the evaluations of both individuals.

In community-based after-school programs, the director likely reports to a board of directors or private owners. Each organizational structure will look different. If an evaluation process is not in place, develop it, schedule it and ensure that the board completes it.

In any evaluation process, your superiors should reflect on your job performance as outlined in your job description. Strengths and weaknesses should be discussed and strategies for improvement determined with specific timelines. An evaluation should be viewed as a positive, summative learning experience. Evaluations should document the quality of your work. They can become valuable records if you come under attack from board members with a negative agenda.

TIP 92

Find a **Mentor**

Most everyone can conjure up a memory of a favorite teacher, community or family member or friend who greatly influenced his or her life in a positive and intimate way. Those relationships dramatically impact and often change young people's lives in outstanding ways. Mentors play important roles for people and professional leaders of any age.

There are times when you will feel the anxious urge to talk about an issue or problem and you won't want anyone you work with to know about your concern. You need a confidant or trusted friend with whom you can bare your soul. Mentors love learning and helping their mentees grow and achieve beyond expectations. Mentors have wisdom to share and a passion to care.

Mentoring is a partnership. It requires time and an intentional commitment to share learning experiences by both individuals. Effective mentoring partnerships are characterized by trust, generosity, truth, commitment, acceptance, patience, frankness, courage, passion and love. You are fortunate if you share those interpersonal characteristics with many individuals, especially your spouse. But with those characteristics and more, a professional mentor uniquely understands the demands and challenges of your job, yet has no direct supervisor connection to your work. Mentors simply commit to guiding, teaching, coaching and helping you become the best you can be at what you do.

Mentors are recognized for having achieved success and outstanding accomplishments in their field and their willingness to teach others. Look around. Build a strong relationship with a mentor. Together, you will learn and gain support to lead after-school learning communities.

TIP 93

Create a **Portfolio or Annual Report**

Educators maintain documentation of their work and help students learn how to show evidence of their learning through the development of portfolios. The collaborative work of principals and after-school program directors should be recorded in a similar manner.

An after-school program's annual report might include:

- the vision and mission statements;
- enrollment statistics;
- program components and content features, reviews and assessments;
- historical development;
- partnership highlights;.
- volunteer and mentoring reports;
- financial reports;
- program evaluation reports;
- synthesis of growth and progress reports;
- recognition of challenges and obstacles;
- letters from the principal and after-school program director;
- statement of future direction and goals;
- pictures; and
- graphs and charts to clarify and accentuate specific points.

Tell your story. Show evidence of student learning, program progress and achievement of goals. The process of collecting and cataloging data for a portfolio or annual report will help you maintain focus on your goals. Publish your annual report on the Web as well as in a professional format on paper. Develop a summary of the portfolio into a PowerPoint presentation that can be placed on DVD. Celebrate your progress and share the success of your collaboration with others.

TIP 94

Integrate Your Program
Into All Policy Decisions

The collaboration between a principal and after-school program director is at a high level when both partners consistently demonstrate awareness and perspective about how their decisions can affect school and after-school links. In particular, this means that principals convey to parents, school staff members, school boards, policymakers, funders, community partners and other key constituents that after-school programs are not a luxury but an integral part of the seamless learning experiences they are striving to provide for all children. Likewise, it means that after-school program directors work closely with the principal to assure that decisions complement the school day.

Moreover, working as a team, principals and after-school program directors use the credibility of their leadership positions to advocate for after-school program availability for all students. They research how policy issues and grants can impact and enhance both their programs. They work to provide a continuum of services and develop a shared message to convey to stakeholders. They work to develop and sustain partnerships that support students and staff members in the school and the after-school program.

TIP 95

Conduct and Participate in
Research Projects

Don't miss opportunities to collect unique forms of data and feedback by participating in research projects and professional studies. The field of after-school education is rapidly growing and ripe for a variety of research projects and dissertation studies. Arrange whatever permissions might be necessary to facilitate a college or university research project, then reap the benefits of the findings. You might consider research topics such as:

- factors that affect principal/after-school-program collaboration;
- the benefits children gain from after-school participation;
- factors that influence mentoring partnerships between volunteers and children in after-school programs;
- funding sources for after-school programs;
- legislative policies that promote and support after-school programs;
- factors that affect and promote positive parent engagement practices;
- environmental factors that affect after-school programs;
- efforts that affect quality;
- the affect of after-school in various settings (urban, suburban, rural);
- obstacles to expanding after-school programs in middle and high schools;
- benefits of summer programs;
- the affect of the development of students' personal and social skills in after-school programs; and
- parent perceptions of the after-school program.

TIP 96

Build **Alliances**

You hear it everywhere: It is important to network to achieve success! That is a good practice, but go further and build alliances.

A professional network helps you connect with other people, especially those who do what you do. But when your school or your center is faced with closure, or your job is being threatened, you need an alliance of professional colleagues, influential community members and trusted friends who will be willing to step forward, stand by your side and help fight your fight.

As leaders, effective principals and after-school program directors possess many competencies and resources that aid them in what they do well. To build alliances, which are partnerships that stretch beyond a professional network, leaders must form relationships with key individuals in their community whose personal competencies and resources, when shared, will become mutually beneficial. Alliances are connections that bring people together in ways that are bigger, better and stronger than a professional network. To move your professional agenda forward, you will need support from an alliance of key community constituents, not just a network of colleagues scattered across diverse locations. Alliances create leverage. Networks simply help people communicate with one another, share information and learn.

You can't build effective alliances if there is anything about you as a person that gets in the way of your interactions with other people. Alliances are built between people of integrity — more than talent or ability. Integrity is truth and honor.

Work to make sure the leaders of your community know you well as an honorable and trustworthy advocate for children.

Build a Professional Library

Invest in professional reading material. Share what you read and own with your collaborative partner. Collect the professional journals that you will receive as part of your membership in state and national professional associations. Buy books. Allow them to be shared by those who work in your after-school program.

Likewise, develop a professional library and resource area for parents. Stock it with pamphlets, a variety of magazines, videos, DVDs and other educational materials that can be shared with parents. Help reduce the incidence of childhood obesity by providing resources that parents can use in their home. Videos and DVDs work best and will be used more often than print materials for children and families from poverty.

The U.S. Department of Education offers a variety of free publications that you should order for your professional resource library and are very appropriate for sharing with parents and stakeholders. To learn more, visit www.edpubs.ed.gov.

Work together and determine titles of books that you and your partner should read and stock on your shelves.

TIP 98

Learn to
Role with the Punches

Principals and after-school program directors must have broad shoulders and let things roll off their backs. As you grow professionally, you'll each experience something that will teach you what that means.

This advice is important as principals and after-school program directors work together. There will be days when one person will say something, give a look or reverse a decision that will offend or challenge the partner. Learn to step back, consider other points of view and let some things go. Pick your battles. The quality of your working relationship is more important than controlling or winning every argument.

Likewise, the rules or the regulations you must abide by to operate an after-school program will change. Special programs will be arranged quickly by outsiders that conflict with and affect the after-school program. A parent will get upset and pull a promising young child from the program. Space that a school district had available for the after-school program one year may not be available another. Never be afraid to confront issues and ask clarifying questions, but learn to accept what you cannot change and move on. To survive as a professional, you must have resiliency. You must be able to recover from insults, put-downs and oversights and to cope with adversity.

There are two types of factors that affect any job — risk and protective. Risk factors tend to exacerbate your vulnerability and increase the likelihood of negative outcomes. Protective factors have an insulating effect and are predictive of positive outcomes. Your ability to increase levels of competence is a key protective factor in building resilience.

Be flexible. Accommodate the needs of others, but don't be a pushover. When the punches come so frequently that you can't handle the pressure of your job, know when to get out.

TIP 99

Empower
Others

"Nine-tenths of education is encouragement."
— *Anatole France*

Don't try to be the hero and do everything yourself. Experience has proven that development is not permanent and change does not have a real impact if it comes from the top down. Principals diminish the effects of their collaboration with after-school program directors and cast a shadow of distrust when they fail to share responsibilities. After-school program directors fail to maximize the potential of staff members when they focus on weaknesses instead of developing strengths.

Empowerment also can be called shared decision-making. Principals and after-school program directors must establish a professional relationship that embodies a sense of efficacy, success and self-worth. They must extend that relationship to those they work with. When educators work for an authoritarian leader, they become bored, resentful and unhappy. To empower each other and your staff members, you must:

- teach expectations and demonstrate desired outcomes;
- provide resources and information needed to do assigned work;
- ensure that the work others are empowered to do is meaningful with sufficient challenges;
- allow time for others to solve problems;
- create a climate of trust and open communication;
- share responsibility and authority;
- provide support, feedback and coaching;
- treat people as individuals and encourage their strengths; and
- help others determine ways to measure their performance.

The keys to empowerment are to clearly teach expectations, allow time, exercise patience and make others feel that their thoughts and opinions are valid and important. Empowerment mobilizes others to embrace the vision of the organization.

TIP 100

Enhance and Develop Your
Communication Style

Principals and after-school program directors who are great talkers share the following communication characteristics:
- They talk about issues with different points of view.
- They influentially convey knowledge and opinions about a variety of issues using language levels understood by the listener.
- They are passionate and enthusiastic.
- They don't talk about themselves all the time. They listen.
- They are curious.
- They empathize.
- They have a sense of humor.
- They have their own style of talking.

Look at issues from different points of view.
Administrative team meetings (or any meeting for that matter) are boring and/or ineffective when participants lack different points of view. Progress and innovation are minimal when "group think" attitudes emerge or if participants lack creativity to mastermind various angles of thinking. Concerned parents quickly dismiss the principal or after-school program director who fails to consider their point of view. Those who lack the ability to identify and present all variables with parents fail to move conversations in desirable ways. People who only possess simple linear thinking are dull.

Convey knowledge and opinions about a variety of issues.
Beyond simply considering different points of view, principals and after-school program directors who talk effectively also have knowledge, expertise and opinions on a variety of issues. They have learned from their

mentors, personal experience, study and interacting with people of their professional network. They have gained sophistication in the profession by seeking knowledge in a variety of ways: listening, reading, writing and interacting in professional development activities with numerous people. They are well-rounded people, capable of discussing current educational issues in professional circles, or sports, entertainment or politics in social settings.

Display passion and enthusiasm.
Leaders who love what they do have a greater chance of creating effective change. Those who really love their jobs project that enthusiasm to others. Those who try to fake enthusiasm fail. The demands of leadership are ever changing and steadily increasing. Parents have little confidence in a leader who is negative, cynical or burned out in the job. Principals or after-school program directors who have lost their enthusiasm for certain aspects of the work must refocus on those things they are passionate about: children, learning, curriculum or serving others. To be effective talkers — and to lead change — they must be able to draw on their passions and persuade the listener to understand them.

Draw others into conversations and listen to them.
Behind their backs, people describe principals or after-school program directors who talk only about themselves as being egotistical and arrogant. In any good conversation, give-and-take sharing occurs between the parties. When one dominates, the other shuts down. Leaders who are good talkers are those who skillfully ask questions that draw others into the conversation. Many people view the principal as an authority figure causing them (especially children) to take a subordinate position in conversations. Observers will consider a principal to be an effective talker when simple questions are asked that engage others and the conversation is balanced.

Be curious.
Principals and after-school program directors who are effective talkers read. They think. They write, and they know how to succinctly put their thoughts together using language at a level that their listeners understand. They are always learning something. They model learning for others. Rather than viewing new initiatives as "just one more thing to do," they welcome new ideas and know how to talk about their learning interests with their listeners.

Show empathy.
People enjoy working with leaders who relate to what they are feeling as well as what they are saying. Leaders who are the best conversationalists are able to commiserate. Focusing on how people feel helps the principal or after-school program director draw others out and open a conversation. It helps develop trust and connectedness. Empathetic leaders know

how to listen and ask questions that show they care, convey recognition and value and show respect for the individual.

Humor.

Never allow yourself to be serious for too long. Humor is everywhere, and principals and after-school program directors who are the best talkers know how to effectively integrate it in conversations. But like enthusiasm, humor doesn't work if it's forced. Everyone will have a unique style of humor, and it must be worked into a conversation naturally. Timing is everything. Leaders who are great talkers enjoy hearing good jokes, see the funny side of things and have a ready repertoire of stories and jokes they can share — naturally, at the right time in conversations.

Train Board Members for
Effective Governance Roles

Governing a complex organization is no easy task. Board members must possess knowledge, skills, experience, courage and character to be effective contributors to their organization. They must bring their talents to the table, do their part, and work as a team in the best interests of the organization. The roles and responsibilities have many similarities. Collectively and individually, school board members as well as those who govern non-profits share roles and responsibilities as outlined in Figure 101a (available at www.schoolagenotes.com).

The principal and after-school program director can help lead volunteer boards when they work closely together to provide orientation training, support, and clarity of vision and mission. Many people will agree to serve if they understand what they are being asked to do and how they can contribute to the mission. The sample job description in Figure 101b (available at www.schoolagenotes.com) can be used as model to help provide that clarity of purpose and role.

Interviewing Program Director Candidates

After-school programs are envisioned and governed in diverse ways. Because of that, various individuals (school-based and community-based, experienced and not) have authority and responsibility for interviewing, selecting and hiring an after-school-program director. For school-based after-school programs, the principal should play a lead role in the selection process.

The written inquiries in this section are suggested to help interviewers prepare their own questions. They are recommendations intended to help leaders identify other leaders with whom they can establish a collaborative partnership that will support the development of a high quality after-school program. Likewise, applicants for after-school program leadership positions may benefit and better prepare by reviewing a sampling of potential interview questions.

General Inquiry (modify to meet your needs)
- Describe your background, high school and college training, and how you got to this point in your career.
- What required training/licensure/certifications do you possess?
- To which professional associations do you belong or would like to belong?
- Describe the last conference, workshop, seminar or class that you attended. Describe the best and worst experiences.
- What community involvement do you have?

Professional Experience
- Describe your professional experience, especially any work in after-school programs.
- Describe your vision of what a high quality after-school program should look like after three years.
- Describe your experience working with parents/volunteers/at-risk students/staff members.
- Have you ever resigned from a job? Been asked to resign? Been dismissed? Explain.
- Why are you leaving or interested in leaving your job?
- Besides what was listed in your last job description, what other responsibilities have you assumed?

Program Quality and Content
- What would you do to establish after-school program content and curriculum and ensure quality?
- What are the national standards for after-school programming?
- What are the state licensure requirements for after-school programming?
- What are some key components of quality after-school programs?
- What would parents/visitors see and hear that would assure them of quality programming?
- What strategies would you implement to assure school/after-school alignment?
- How would you promote the after-school program?
- How should an after-school program be evaluated?
- If you have limited experience, what resources or people would you access to better understand program standards, quality and content?

Work Initiative
- How willing are you to work a contract job vs. hourly wage?
- Do you have commitments that would prevent you from attending meetings/workshops, etc., outside your work hours?
- Describe what you read for professional growth.
- How would you describe your personal code of ethics?

Student/People Management
- Do you distinguish between discipline and punishment?
- Describe a proper atmosphere for an after-school program.
- What rules would you implement in an after-school program?
- Describe two or three problems/issues you would handle that developed in the after-school program and two or three you feel the principal should/must handle.
- How does structure relate to student/adult management in an after-school program?

Program Leadership

- Describe your experience and success in writing grants.
- Describe your capacity to work with technology: computers, the Internet, Web sites, digital cameras, etc.
- Describe your experience in working with budgeting and program accountability.
- What are some myths about after-school programming that you would work to dispel?
- How do you react to conflict? How do you handle stress?
- How do others describe your leadership abilities? What descriptors do they use? Why?
- How do you create an effective team among after-school personnel?
- How would you facilitate communication between school staff and the after-school program staff?
- How do you define collaboration? Describe what you think works and what doesn't in a collaborative partnership?

Summary

- What makes you the best candidate for this leadership position?
- Who are your professional references?
- What hasn't been asked or talked about that you want to share?
- What questions does the candidate have? (Look for quality, interest and unique insights).

Conclusion

To improve the quality of the intellectual endeavor of collaboration, principals and after-school program directors must be willing to examine their leadership skills, personal and professional competencies, knowledge and commitment to the partnership with a critical eye. Creating a quality after-school program requires participants to reflect — alone and together. Collaborative partners share a willingness to improve, a capacity to change and a belief in successful outcomes for all participants. Moreover, principals and after-school program directors who 'get it right' understand and embrace the idea that improving the quality of their partnership is an ongoing process.

It is upon this idea of getting it right that this book is structured. Its contents are based upon the experience, knowledge, research and documentation of principals and after-school practitioners from across the country. The result, I hope, is a tool that can be used to promote continuous improvement of key aspects of collaboration. The self-assessment tools, available online at www.schoolagenotes.com, are provided to begin the ongoing process of reflection. As you read and reflect, you may conclude that your collaboration and job performance skills are adequately aligned with the tips and advice in this book. That's great, and congratulations. Now, I challenge you to add more and share your ideas and advice with practitioners in the field. Working together, practitioners can define 'real world' best practices of collaboration and after-school programming.

To develop your collaborative partnership, start with a discussion and creation of a vision. Talk about it. Write about it. Speak about it. Let your passion become contagious and spread to others. Your vision of an extended learning day for children should include many ideas that, when your efforts are fully realized, will enhance student learning and increase achievement. Nothing will happen without a shared vision.

Next, get organized and build a solid infrastructure. An after-school program that is organized and well structured can attain standards of quality — but not without a clear vision from its leaders. Never lose focus on the little things that collectively make a big difference.

Leaders never stop learning. They take good care of themselves, personally and professionally. Collaborators never stop learning. They work as a team and share responsibility for success.

The fact that you've read this book and discussed its contents shows that you care about working as part of a collaborative team and understand the importance of continuous communication to 'get it right.'

Web Resources

Afterschool Alliance — http://www.afterschoolalliance.org/
A nonprofit organization dedicated to raising awareness of the importance of after-school programs and advocating for quality, affordable programs for all children. It is supported by a group of public, private and nonprofit organizations that share the Alliance's vision of ensuring that all children have access to after-school programs by 2010.

Afterschool.gov — http://www.afterschool.gov/
This site connects after-school providers to federal resources that support children and youth during out-of-school hours.

AfterschoolPRO.net — http://www.afterschoolpro.net/
This group provides links to organizations, agencies and resource lists, and provides a calendar of conferences and events. Add your name to the AfterSchool Professional Network (free) and participate in special interest exchanges and enjoy member benefits.

The After-School Corporation — http://www.tascorp.org/
This New York-based organization works nationally to enhance the quality, availability and sustainability of comprehensive, daily after-school programs. The first nonprofit organization in the nation to set about building a citywide K-12 after-school system, TASC funds, monitors, evaluates and supports after-school programs in New York City public schools.

C.S. Mott Foundation — http://www.mott.org/ourissues/Afterschool.aspx
Based in Flint, Michigan, this private foundation supports grants that strengthen the after-school field through technical assistance, research, evaluation and policy development, and by building public support.

Collaborative Communications — http://www.collaborativecommunications.com/content/index.php?pid=1
A communications consulting practice that forms partnerships with national foundations, the public sector, nonprofit education and commu-

nity-based organizations and school districts to create initiatives, distinctive products and sustainable solutions that can improve the performance of groups serving public education.

Center for Afterschool and Community Education at Foundations Inc. — http://www.caceafterschool.org
CACE provides integrated professional development, program content publications and technical assistance designed to support and enhance the diversity of programs, leaders and staff members who are transforming the lives of children and youth.

The Finance Project — http://www.financeproject.org/
A specialized nonprofit research, consulting, technical assistance and training firm for public and private sector leaders nationwide.

Learning Points Associates — http://www.learningpt.org
Learning Point Associates helps schools and districts plan, create and evaluate strong after-school programs.

National AfterSchool Association — http://www.naaweb.org/
The leading voice of the after-school profession dedicated to the development, education and care of children and youth during their out-of-school hours.

National Association of Elementary School Principals — http://www.naesp.org/
The mission of NAESP is to lead in the advocacy and support for elementary and middle level principals and other education leaders in their commitment to all children.

National Institute on Out-of-School Time — http://www.niost.org/
NIOST's mission is to ensure that all children, youth and families have access to high quality programs, activities and opportunities during non-school hours.

School-Age NOTES — http://www.schoolagenotes.com
For more than 29 years, directors and staff of after-school programs from around the world have come to rely on School-Age NOTES as a trusted provider of high quality, innovative resources and training.

U.S. Department of Education — http://www.ed.gov/programs/21stcclc/index.html
21st Century Community Learning Centers — This program supports the creation of community learning centers that provide academic enrichment opportunities during non-school hours for children, particularly students who attend high-poverty and low-performing schools.

Recommended Readings

Afterschool Alliance. (2005). Arts and Afterschool: A Powerful Combination. Issue Brief No. 21; http://www.afterschoolalliance.org//issue_21_arts_cfm

A New Day for Learning. http://www.newdayforlearning.org

Arizona Board of Regents (2005). The benefits of walking. http://lifework.arizona.edu/wsw/walking/benefits.php; Retrieved February 16, 2008.

benShea, N. (2000). *What every principal would like to say ... and what to say next time.* Thousand Oaks, CA: Corwin Press, Inc.

Blaydes, J. (2003). *The educator's book of quotes.* Thousand Oaks, CA: Corwin Press, Inc.

Bodilly, S. & Beckett, M. (2005). *Making out-of-school time matter.* Santa Monica, CA: RAND Corporation.

Brinkman, R. & Kirschner, R. (2006). *Dealing with difficult people.* New York: McGraw-Hill Companies, Inc.

Brown, J. (2006). *The imperfect board member: Discovering the seven disciplines of governance excellence.* San Francisco: Jossey-Bass.

Carlson, M., & Donohoe, M. (2003). *The executive director's survival guide.* San Francisco: John Wiley & Sons, Inc. (Jossey-Bass).

Fagan, J. (2003). Extended learning for children of poverty. *Principal, 82* (5), p. 26.

Godin, S. (2003). *The purple cow.* New York: The Penguin Group.

Halpern, R. (2002). A Different Kind of Child Development Institution: The History of After-School Programs for Low-Income Children. *Teacher's College Record, 104* (2). p. 178-211.

Johnson, R. and Johnson, D. (1988). Cooperative Learning. Transforming Education. *In Context, 18.* p 34.

Kouzes, J. & Posner, B. (1995). *The leadership challenge.* San Francisco: Jossey-Bass.

Lockwood, A. (2008). *The principal's guide to afterschool programs.* Thousand Oaks, CA: Corwin Press, Inc.

Marx, G. (2000). *Ten trends: Educating children for a profoundly different future.* Arlington, VA: Educational Research Service.

Maxwell, J. (2003). *Attitude 101.* Nashville: Thomas Nelson, Inc.

Maxwell, J. (2002). *Leadership 101.* Nashville: Thomas Nelson, Inc

National Afterschool Association (1998). *The NAA standards for quality school-age care.* Boston: National Afterschool Association.

National Association of Elementary School Principals (2006). *Leading after-school learning communities.* Alexandria, VA: author.

National Association of Elementary School Principals (2005). *Making the most of after-school time.* Alexandria, VA: author.

Noam, G. (2003). After-School Education: What Principals Should Know. *Principal, 82* (5), p. 19-21.

Owens, D. & Vallercamp, N. (2003). Eight Keys to a Successful Expanded-Day Program. *Principal, 82* (5), p. 23-25.

Payne, R., DeVol, P., & Smith, T. (2001). *Bridges out of poverty.* Highlands, TX: aha!Process, Inc.

Payne, R. (2005). *A framework for understanding poverty.* Highlands, TX; aha!Process, Inc.

Ricken, R., Terc, M. & Ayres, I. (2001). *The elementary school principal's calendar.* Thousand Oaks, CA: Corwin Press.

Rinehart, J. (2003). A New Day Begins After School. *Principal, 82* (5), p. 12-16.

U.S. Department of Agriculture (2008). MyPyramid.gov. http://www.mypyramid.gov/global_nav/about.html

Young, P. (2008). *Promoting positive behaviors: An elementary principal's guide to structuring the learning environment.* Thousand Oaks, CA: Corwin Press.

Young, P. (2004). *You have to go to school, you're the principal: 101 tips to make it better for your students, your staff, and yourself.* Thousand Oaks, CA: Corwin Press.